AN HOUR *in* T*h*E GARDEN

*ded*ɪcaᴛɪoɴ. For Sue Stubbs, the photographer, who has become not only a great collegue but also a friend. Thanks for your creative input and beautiful illustrations.

AN HOUR in The GARDEN

Meredith Kirton

Photography by Sue Stubbs

MURDOCH BOOKS

CONTENTS

INTRODUCTION

Gardening is one of those crafts that for many has skipped a generation. The post-World War II era of modern conveniences and outsourcing (now the mower man perhaps does your lawn and most of us no longer need to grow food in the backyard) has meant that getting your hands dirty and 'communing with nature' have passed many by.

Instead of being passed on from parent to child, years of accumulated knowledge have disappeared, and the new generation of gardeners struggle to get a grip on simple techniques and garden tasks. But just because many of us have not learned how to garden or grow our own food doesn't mean that we don't want to. This book is meant to be a hands-on, illustrated glossary of ideas and methods that you will find indispensable if you're just beginning to discover the joys of gardening.

START SMALL

As with any other craft, don't attempt to leap in the deep end with a mammoth transformation ... after all, you knit a scarf before attempting a cardigan. Potter about with small projects till your confidence and ability grow. Try looking through the 'Pocket-sized projects' section for inspiration, starting off with simple table decorations and 'just add water' ideas and working your way up to those that need more patience, such as the espaliered camellia. If edible plants are more your thing, try growing your own, from a herb tower to an edible flower salad — there are ideas to suit everyone's tastes and abilities. Once you've mastered these, why not explore the further reaches of the garden, with garden ventures. These are all laid out like a recipe book, with all the ingredients, processes and aftercare ideas and alternatives shown in simple step-by-step detail. Many of these ideas are perfect for courtyard and balcony gardeners, but would work equally well for those of you with your own backyard.

MASTERING THE BASICS

If you have just bought your own home for the first time, or finally decided to immerse yourself in the garden, there are many jobs to do in order to get the best from your patch. Breaking them down into one hour tasks demystifies the whole process, and makes maintenance seem much more enjoyable and less complicated. The 'Taken to task' section will guide you through most garden maintenance, from recycling and composting to pruning, lawn care, the dreaded chore of weeding and garden organization.

CORNER TRANSFORMATIONS

Once you have a handle on some of the basics, it's time to launch yourself into more serious work. Making over the worst corner of your plot is a great way to make a big impact with minimal effort and cost. The simple ideas contained within the 'Mini makeovers' section are not supposed to tax your finances or your skills. They are simple ideas to transform the ugly into the desirable and provide inspiration for your own creations. Many of the makeovers contain a few different small projects, but show how these 'recipes' can be used as a 'pièce de résistance' for a total look. From a covered verandah to the 'outside room', a beachside makeover or just a folly to bring a smile to your face, there is something for everyone!

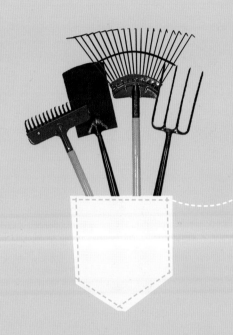

POCKET-SIZED PROJECTS

SIMPLE IDEAS FOR THE BUDDING GARDENER

DECORATING WITH PLANTS

One way of starting out with plants, especially when you don't have much time, is to think of them as just another item that can be used for decoration. Just as you would put new covers on your cushions from time to time, perhaps even changing your soft furnishings with the seasons, you may wish to change the look of your garden. Gardening need not be a lifetime commitment if you don't want it to be. Just have fun experimenting with plants, using them as table pieces and even living sculptures.

None of the projects in this section takes more than an hour to make, but all of them will provide you with weeks, or even months, of enjoyment.

CUT FLOWERS

In days gone by, large homes were supported by a staff who grew not only produce for the kitchen, but also flowers for harvesting as cut flowers. These dedicated cut-flower beds must have been a great joy to behold, with rows of zinnias, dahlias and asters for summer blooms, and trellises of sweet peas, beds of stock and of course, rows of bulbs for cuttings. Today, many bulbs are still grown for cut flower production, with tulips, Dutch iris and other breathtaking blooms produced and then sold in the world's flower markets.

You certainly don't need a home of grand proportions to enjoy the beauty of flowers in your home, but if your budget doesn't stretch to a weekly visit to the florist, consider having some cutting flowers around your garden, either in among the shrubbery, as part of the shrubbery itself, brightening up a vegie patch, or even in pots which can then either be brought indoors flowering or picked for a vase.

HANDY HINT.

Many summer and autumn flowering bulbs are from warmer climates such as South Africa. They include stunners such as the gloriosa lily (*Gloriosa superba*) (see below), the incredibly tough and drought-tolerant crinum lilies (*Crinum moorei* and *C. bulbispermum*), and the beautiful red fire lily (*Vallota speciosa*).

Cut blooms when they are still in bud, but just showing some colour, and put into water straight away — carry a bucket with you. This will prolong their vase life considerably, and is one of the advantages of growing your own cut flowers.

STUNNING APRICOT-COLOURED TULIPS

VIBRANT DARK BLUE DUTCH IRIS

FRAGRANT YELLOW FREESIAS

THE EXQUISITELY PERFUMED TUBEROSE

MULTI-STOREY BULBS

It's not always easy to be inspired by those onion-like things in net bags that appear in garden centres each autumn. They look too much like hard work to fit into today's garden, so too often they are overlooked or disregarded.

But bulbs are worth the wait and the effort. Indeed, half the joy of bulbs is that they are ephemeral, for in that fleeting moment there is delight. The problem is that we want more than one flower from each bulb, and most of the time that's all we get — so for greater pizzazz try double-stacking for double the effect!

YOU WILL NEED.

Up to 25 bulbs, of 5 or 6 different types

A standard 25 cm (10 in) pot

Potting mix (compost) with a high organic content (you can buy specially formulated bulb mixes, or add some extra peat to a standard blend)

STEP 1

STEP 2

STEP 3

STEP 4

S T E P   1   As a rule of thumb, the greater the diameter of the bulb, the deeper it needs to be planted. Following this principle, hyacinths and daffodils should go in at the bottom of your pot. Spread 10 cm (4 in) or so of potting mix (compost) at the base of your pot and evenly space your first layer of bulbs.

S T E P   2   Spread another layer of potting mix over the first bulbs, then, being careful not to plant directly above the bulbs in the first layer, plant your next largest bulbs, Dutch iris and tulips for example.

S T E P   3   Keep on building up the potting mix till the tips of the bulbs in the second layer are practically covered. Then, again not planting directly above the bulbs in either the base layer or the middle layer, plant your smallest bulbs — freesia, triteleia, ranunculus and anemone all fall into this category.

S T E P   4   Cover this final layer over with potting mix, and dress with a layer of sphagnum moss, or even grass seeds or annuals such as alyssum and lobelia. The result is spectacular!

GARdeNeR's Tips.   The multi-storey approach can be varied in a number of ways, and is just as successful for pockets in a rockery as for pots. Group early, mid-season and late-flowering bulb varieties to extend the period of colour up to 100 days.

Use a variety of colours as I have done here to create a rainbow of colour, or choose bulbs all in one colour to create a dramatic splash. For extra floral value, plant ranunculus — they produce up to 28 blooms per corm!

DIVINE LILIES

Lilies are among the most glorious flowers known. One type was held in such high esteem that it was named after the Virgin Mary (the madonna lily, *Lilium candidum*) and nurtured carefully as it travelled right around the world from its native habitat in the countries of the eastern Mediterranean. Today lilies are grown for their exquisite beauty, luscious fragrance and long life as cut flowers. To bring a little bit of heaven to your place, why not pot them up into a container so you can bring them inside for greater appreciation when they bloom?

Once the flowers start to fade, take the pot outside into the sun so that the bulbs can store up enough energy to flower again the next year.

STEP 1

STEP 2

STEP 3

STEP 1   Lily bulbs need to be stored carefully as they don't have a tough outer skin like some other bulbs (such as onions and daffodils). They mostly come stored in wood shavings or peat moss. If you plan on keeping bulbs from last season, store them in brown paper bags. If you have lilies in several colours, it's a good idea to keep them in separately labelled bags.

STEP 2   Put sufficient potting mix (compost) into the pot to give the bulbs a thick enough layer to send out a good root system.

STEP 3   Ascertain which end of the bulb is the top and which is the bottom. There may be an obvious shoot indicating new growth (but not always). This goes up! The best gauge is normally the roots — remnants will still be attached somewhere, so make sure these are pointing down.

YOU WILL NEED.

Premium potting mix (compost) with soil wetter and fertilizer already mixed in. Check it has the relevant standards marking (5 ticks in Australia) so that it holds water well and is easy to re-wet if it becomes dry.

6 bulbs of the *Lilium orientale* hybrid, cultivars 'Star Gazer' (pink) and 'Casablanca' (white) are used here

Moss

STEP 4

STEP 5

STEP 6

STEP 4   Plant lilies in groups for maximum effect, 8 cm (3¼ in) deep in a rich bulb potting mix that contains plenty of slow-release fertilizer and organic matter. Mix up the bulbs if you are using different colours so that they flower in a random pattern. Here dark pink and white lilies are used.

STEP 5   Backfill with more potting mix, but don't tamp it down too firmly, as lilies like an airy, friable soil.

STEP 6   Mulching with moss will help keep the bulbs moist, and improve the overall look of the container while they are dormant. The emerging shoots will easily penetrate the moss.

STEP 7   Lilies like to stay moist and well fed, but a common mistake is to water the bulbs too often before they start to grow, which can lead to rot. The best advice here is to water them once when you pot them, then wait patiently for the shoots to appear, at which point you can resume watering.

STEP 7

GARdeNeR'S TiP.   If you want to use your lilies as cut flowers, always leave a section of stem with some leaves at the base when you cut them so the bulb can still grow and perform for you next year.

DAFFODIL BULBS

Growing bulbs for indoor display is a great way of bringing the garden indoors. Daffodils provide a lovely, fresh and fun spring feeling, and using kitchen containers as pots is a nice twist. Shown here are old pudding basins, which work especially well in the kitchen and living areas. Other options for containers include ceramic bowls, or cut crystal from your granny's dressing table, which are particularly nice for bedroom display. If you don't like the look of bare earth around the stems, consider seeding some lawn grass at the same time, to add a green carpet, or planting moss or baby's tears (*Soleirolia*) as a living ground cover.

STEP 1   Because these bulbs are going to be grown in pots without drainage holes, it's important to line the base with 5 cm (2 in) or so of gravel for drainage.

STEP 2   Place 3–4 bulbs on top of the gravel, so that their roots will grow down into the water reservoir in the gravel.

STEP 3   Surround your bulbs with potting mix (compost) and water them sparingly so that the potting mix is just moist.

STEP 1   STEP 2   STEP 3

GAR*dene*R'S T*i*P. Make sure that the bulbs don't ever become more than just moist, any wetter and they will rot.

SUCCULENTS IN POTS

Succulents are in the midst of a huge resurgence in popularity. They are so much in favour that in many gardens there are more succulents than traditional flowering plants, especially in gardens with space restrictions or in hot, dry areas.

Plants that can cope with drought are proving themselves invaluable. Succulents are cousins to cacti, but fortunately they don't come armed with thorns. Instead, they have thick fleshy leaves. They come in a stunning array of shapes and colours and, best of all, they are easy to grow.

Succulents will strike, or reproduce, easily from virtually any part of the plant, even a single leaf. A new rosette will form at the base of the leaf, feeding off the old leaf until it has rooted and is able to sustain itself. They will also grow from larger pieces and stem cuttings. Gather a range of succulents from friends and willing neighbours to start your own garden or potted collection.

Your new 'friendship garden' is sure to survive long after you have moved on, such is the staying power of succulents.

STEP 1

STEP 2

STEP 3

S T E P   1   Gather some cuttings together and put them in a dry spot protected from rain. Cuttings and leaves from succulents, like these echeveria leaves, need to dry out for a few weeks before planting, which helps form a callus over any wounds and thus stops fungal attacks.

S T E P   2   Once they have callused over, you'll start to see small rootlets appear, and even tiny rosettes of foliage, at the base of each leaf. Gently tuck the leaves with the rosettes into a bed of free-draining potting mix. Keep out of strong sunlight at this stage.

S T E P   3   Once they have all rooted well and formed into larger plants, lift and plant out into larger pots or in the garden. The more sun available, the better the shape and colour will be on the plant. Mulch with pebbles to help reduce under-plant humidity and keep weeds down to a minimum. It looks great too! Water lightly after one week.

YOU WILL NEED.

Cuttings from a friend, or from a 'mother plant' of your own

Cactus and succulent potting mix (compost), which has more sand and grit than regular mix

Seedling tray with divided cells, or any container with divisions

Terracotta pots; these are 15 cm (6 in) squat pots

Crushed gravel for mulch

GARDENER'S TIP.   After a year the potting mix (compost) will start to become depleted of its nutrients. At this stage establish a regular feeding pattern. Only use low-nitrogen slow-release granular fertilizers or a quality low-nitrogen liquid fertilizer.

STRING OF PEARLS

The delightful string of pearls (*Senecio rowleyanus*), a mat-forming succulent from the Eastern Cape in South Africa, has unusual cinnamon-scented flowers and looks for all the world like a collection of Art Deco jade bead necklaces. Finding a pot fit for such an elegant plant is no easy task. Go for something with aged grace, like the cast iron urn featured here, or a marble or alabaster one.

STEP 1   STEP 2   STEP 3

YOU WILL NEED.

Elegant urn

Potting mix (compost) formulated for cacti and succulents

String of pearls (*Senecio rowleyanus*)

STEP 1   The trick is to be as careful as possible, as the string of pearls falls apart easily. Add some potting mix (compost) to the new container to bring the repotted plant to the correct height. Cautiously upturn the old container, supporting the plant with a gentle hand.

STEP 2   Break the root ball into several chunks.

STEP 3   Position chunks around the urn until it's full, add extra potting mix to fill any empty spaces, and carefully arrange the pearls to hang over the urn.

STEP 4   Water well and display in pride of place.

CHAIN OF HEARTS SPHERE

Chain of hearts (*Ceropegia linearis* subsp. *woodii*) is a charming and unusual trailing plant. It is often used in hanging baskets, where its stunning heart-shaped leaves can cascade down for about 60 cm (2 ft).

It can also be used as a climber, which is the way I have used it here to make a silvery grey sphere. The succulent leaves make it drought hardy and tolerant, a perfect plant for pots.

YOU WILL NEED.

Chain of hearts (*Ceropegia linearis* subsp. *woodii*)

Pot

Potting mix (compost)

Wire coathanger

Newspaper to work on

Pliers

Dustpan and brush for clean-up

STEP 1

STEP 2

STEP 3

STEP 4

STEP 5

STEP 6

STEP 1   The first step is to make a frame. A wire coathanger is easily bent into a rounded shape with four 'ribs' using pliers. Leave the hook in place as an anchor.

STEP 2   Put the frame into the pot, hook down, and half fill with potting mix (compost).

STEP 3   Carefully divide a pot of chain of hearts into four, ensuring each piece has a tuber and some roots.

STEP 4   Position the four sections of plant between the ribs of the sphere, and top up with more potting mix.

STEP 5   Gently wind the trailing stems around the ribs of the frame. From time to time, as the plants grow, repeat this process until the sphere is complete.

STEP 6   Leave for a few weeks before watering. This allows any damaged roots to callus over, reducing the risk of fungal rot.

GARDENER'S TIP. For a charming Saint Valentine's Day gift, swap the sphere for a heart-shaped frame.

LIVING STONES

Living stones, or *Lithops*, as they are known botanically, are succulents which look exactly like pebbles. They are native to dry areas of southern Africa, and have a strangeness about them which is beguiling. For the most part these plants grow underground, and the 'stones' appearing on the surface are a pair of leaves which help protect the underground part of the plant from Africa's incredibly bright sunlight. Each pair of leaves has particular markings, depending on the species, which can vary from spots to stripes and even translucent panes which let you see into the plant's interior. Not always easy to find, but well worth the hunt, *Lithops* are available from specialist cactus and succulent nurseries. They need watering only sparingly, will cope with air-conditioning and, naturally, extreme heat. What they won't tolerate is shade and humidity, nor any winter water. Plant them up into pots and trays, mulch with gravel and have fun playing 'spot the living pebble'!

YOU WILL NEED.

A number of living stones *(Lithops)*

A free-draining container

A free-draining potting mix (compost) specially formulated for succulents and cacti

Pebbled gravel or mulch

STEP 1

STEP 2

STEP 1   To ensure the 'stones' have good drainage, mix some coarse material, like this gravel, into the potting mix (compost).

STEP 2   Plant your 'stones' randomly in the tray.

STEP 3   Mulch with an attractive gravel for a finished look.

GARDENER'S TIP.
Don't be alarmed when your living stones shed their outer skins, in much the same way as a snake. This is how they grow. It's a sure sign that you've made them happy enough to warrant a growth spurt.

JELLY BEAN BOWL

Sedums, or stonecrops as they are also called, come in a variety of colours, shapes and sizes. Some grow as shrubs, but some are low, mounding plants that bear an uncanny likeness to jelly beans. These succulent-leafed plants come in a delicate array of colours, from soft apricot to ruby red and emerald green, with a delicious translucence to them. They also flower, with tiny golden stars each spring smothering new growth. Marry them with a glazed bowl and you have a yummy-looking table decoration. Sedums will colour more with the more sun they receive, so grow them outside in an open sunny spot to allow them to show their true colours.

STEP 1

STEP 2

STEP 1   Gently free the cuttings or seedlings from their pots.

STEP 2   Arrange them artfully in the glazed bowl (making sure it has a drainage hole) and backfill with potting mix (compost). You might like to mulch with white pebbles.

YOU WILL NEED.

A collection of potted sedum seedlings, or make your own (see page 21) from leaf cuttings

Glazed bowl

Free-draining potting mix (compost) for succulents and cacti

White gravel

GARDENER'S TIPS.
They might look like lollies, but many species of sedum are actually used as salad vegetables — or medicinally. So they are definitely not for the sweet tooth!

The common weedy succulent, purslane *(Portulaca oleracea)*, is also edible, and can also be eaten fresh in a salad.

CARNIVOROUS PLANTS

Carnivorous plants are so named because they eat insects, catching them using various dastardly forms of entrapment, then 'eating' the helpless victim by dissolving it in digestive juices. Carnivorous plants come from many parts of the world, but most come from the tropics. They love to be kept moist and thrive in warm, humid conditions.

The most famous of all is, of course, the venus flytrap (*Dionaea muscipula*), which snaps shut on its prey and digests the live insects to add to its nutrient supply. The lesser known, but stunningly beautiful, pitcher plants of the genus *Sarracenia* (one is shown below and to the right) secrete nectar from glands around their hoods. This lures insects down a never-to-escape slippery-slide of death into a fluid that breaks down the insects' tissues.

Australia has its own carnivorous plants, the sundews of the genus *Drosera* (see box on the right), which bind their captives with a sticky honey until all the necessary goodies have dissolved.

Pitcher plants are especially striking-looking plants, and grow anywhere where there is plenty of direct sunshine and regular water, either in a tray or an attractive bowl. Try decorating your windowsill or using them as a table centrepiece.

STEP 1

STEP 2

STEP 3

STEP 1   Plant the taller pitcher plants first. Put a handful of sphagnum moss in the bowl as a base, then carefully put the rootballs on top of it.

STEP 2   Backfill with some more moss, then plant any smaller flytraps or a few sundews.

STEP 3   Water well. Make sure that the pitcher plants are all fully upright and supported by the moss, as they have a tendency to flop — and they'll never get to eat dinner if that happens!

THE CONTRASTING COLOURING OF THE PITCHER PLANT

YOU WILL NEED.

Carnivorous plants

Sphagnum moss

Watertight container or pot with saucer

Atomizer and watering can

HANDY HINT.

Many carnivorous plants, including these sundews, are easily divided to make more 'insect traps'. Do this in winter during their dormancy period.

GARDENER'S TIP. Mist your carnivorous plant with water occasionally to keep the air humid. Cut back any dead growth at the end of winter. Sundews also revel in damp conditions, so you could try revamping a terrarium, an old fishtank or a glass bowl, such as the Victorian-era frilled-edged container in the project on the left.

LIVING WREATH

Yes, a living, growing Christmas wreath is possible, made with the most amazing plants on earth — tillandsias, or air plants. Many have silvery tones and others have pinkish-red centres, making them ideal for Christmas. Almost impossible to kill, they live off nothing but the moisture in the air. Once you've finished with the festivities, hang your wreath up outside somewhere in the shade, perhaps in a tree, and it will keep healthy and happy till next year.

YOU WiLL Need.

A twig wreath. This one is from a craft supplier, but you could make one up yourself from fine twigs, such as willow, fruit tree wood or tea tree, and wire

Spanish moss and an assortment of other tillandsias, available from good garden centres

Screw-in hook for the door

Ribbon or wire to attach the wreath to the hook

Hot glue gun and glue cartridges

Atomizer

STEP 1

STEP 2

STEP 3

STEP 4

STEP 1   Position the tillandsias around your wreath, with any flowers and new growth pointing up to the top of the wreath. Cluster them into groups to show them off to best advantage, placing similar types together, and working in a symmetrical pattern from side to side, bottom to top.

STEP 2   When you are happy with your arrangement, add a drop or two of glue from the hot glue gun to the base of a plant

and gently push it into a niche in the twigs. This holds the plant in place and helps create a realistic effect.

STEP 3   Attach each plant in a similar manner.

STEP 4   Fill in any gaps with Spanish moss and tie a ribbon at the top to hang the wreath. Mist occasionally with an atomizer to help humidify your plants and bring out their best colours.

'JUST ADD WATER'

Lawns could easily become the dinosaurs of outdoor living, with paved areas and decking becoming the new backyard 'floor' treatment. Don't throw the baby out with the bathwater though. Grasses come in many forms, not just as turf. Many ornamental species can work terrifically well mass-planted in the garden, or grown in pots to highlight their best attributes.

This grass is a New Zealand native sedge. Many forms are available, including plain green leaf types, cream-striped forms and this fabulous golden grass, *Acorus gramineus* 'Ogon'. It is a perennial which can be used to brighten pathways, borders and in between paving, in the same way as mondo grass (*Ophiopogon*). It loves a partly shaded, moist position in the garden, but can also be grown in ponds, vases or pots with a saucer of water keeping it damp. Sedges grow as well in water as they do in soil. Plants like these, known as marginals, are often pond fringe-dwellers in their natural habitat. Aquarium shops stock many aquatic plants, but even nurseries sell marginals. *Acorus* is the perfect grass for growing as an ornamental in a vase.

YOU WILL NEED.

A vase — glass or clear plastic so you can still see the roots

Water-storing crystals (see page 135) or ornamental pebbles

Ornamental water-loving grasses, such as this sedge

Hose and watering can

Scissors to trim up leaves and any damaged roots

STEP 1

STEP 2

STEP 3

STEP 4

S T E P   1   Wash off any potting mix (compost) or soil from the roots.

S T E P   2   Using a clean glass container, weight your plant down with decorative pebbles (or water crystals) and position as desired, but make sure there is plenty of natural light.

S T E P   3   Trim any damaged leaves or roots

S T E P   4   Fill the container with water to just cover the roots, but don't cover the blades of grass themselves.

A spare 5 minutes.

AGAVES IN WATER

Sometimes cleaning up in the garden can lead to new planting opportunities. This agave, also known as century plant, tends to brown at the base as plants grow taller, which means they need tidying up. This is simply done by pulling away the dead leaves. Removing side shoots (pups) from the base and striking them in water is a fast and simple way of growing new plants. They also last indoors in water for months and look great on the windowsill.

   If you grow sick of their watery company, plant them out in the garden or into pots, where they grow easily. They make wonderful statement plants beside entranceways.

FLAT-PACK PLANTS: ESPALIER CAMELLIA

Growing plants as espaliers sounds much more complicated than it is. Espalier is simply a technique for space saving, by growing plants flat, against either a wall or frame, so that they still flower and fruit, but don't take up any width. It is an excellent treatment for bare walls, narrow garden beds or ugly fences.

Traditionally, espalier has been used for fruit-bearing plants, but more modern uses include berrying and flowering plants. *Camellia sasanqua*, the autumn-flowering, smaller bloomed camellia, makes an ideal choice. Choose a camellia that already has a two-dimensional shape if you can. Plant it directly into its final destination, either in a pot with a frame, or hard up against a trellised wall.

STEP 1

STEP 2

STEP 3

STEP 1   Trim off any outward-facing branches.

STEP 2   Secure the remaining growth, using budding tape, onto the frame or wall trellis.

STEP 3   As the espaliered plant grows, trim off any outward-facing shoots regularly, tie back the lateral growths and enjoy your flowering wall shrub!

YOU WILL NEED.

Young *Camellia sasanqua*

Pot with frame, or garden bed against a wall with attached frame or trellis wires

Secateurs (garden shears)

Budding tape (grafting tape)

MOSS BALL

Sculpture is a wonderful element to add to the outdoor arena. It can be a work of art from a favourite artist, or an individual piece created by you. Even if you lack confidence in your artistic abilities, you can try growing a living sculpture.

Topiary has been used as living sculpture for centuries, but its downside is that it is high maintenance, and has to be trimmed regularly. This moss ball, which requires no trimming, is a wonderful alternative to topiary. Here I have shown a very simple geometric design, but you might want to do something more elaborate and use the clay to model a nude figure or other folly. Let loose ... after all, whatever your design, it will only improve with age as the moss colonizes and settles in, hiding any faux pas.

This could also be a good project for the kids to help with. Moss can be harvested from the garden, and often clay can be found there too. If not, buy second-grade potter's clay from an art supplier to keep costs down.

YOU WILL NEED.

Heavy plastic for working on

Wire cutters or secateurs
(garden shears)

Chicken wire, or flexible wire mesh
(available from art suppliers)

A fully inflated ball of the
desired size

Potter's clay

Piano wire

Metal hairpins, or make your own
using small pliers and light wire

Old kitchen fork

Moss; perhaps from shady areas in
your garden, otherwise available
from many florists

Atomizer

STEP 1

STEP 2

STEP 1   Using wire cutters for chicken wire, or secateurs for the artist's wire mesh, cut a piece to size. Be generous with the overlap.

STEP 2   To form a template, wrap the chicken wire or flexible wire mesh around a ball similar in size to your desired sphere.

STEP 3

STEP 4

STEP 5

STEP 6

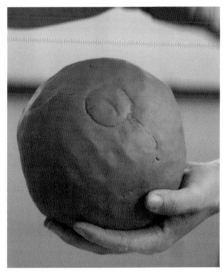

STEP 7

STEP 8

S T E P   3   Slice off an appropriate-sized chunk of potter's clay with piano wire.

S T E P   4   Work the clay into a rough sphere shape.

S T E P   5   Remove the ball from the wire template and replace it with the clay ball. Smooth the wire firmly against the clay, using a couple of hairpins if necessary to keep it in place.

S T E P   6   Cut several 1.5 cm (⅝ in) slices of clay from the original piece and use them to cover the wire with a 'skin'. Work the edges of the slices together and smooth the clay so the sphere has a nicely rounded surface.

S T E P   7   Pat the clay gently with your hands until you have an acceptable shape.

S T E P   8   Roughen the surface with a fork to help the moss bed in the clay.

STEP 9

STEP 10

STEP 11

STEP 9   Using small sections, secure the moss to the clay with the wire hairpins.

STEP 10   Cover the whole surface, leaving no bald patches.

STEP 11   Mist with water. While moss has been around for millions of years, it will need a shady home and regular misting to help it survive the next few weeks until it roots into its clay base.

HANdY HINT.

Moss from your garden may need to be trimmed up and cleaned before you use it.

GARdENER'S TIP.   There are lots of low-growing moss like plants you could use as alternatives — mondo grass *(Ophiopogon)* could be fun as 'hair', baby's tears *(Soleirolia)* could work, as could selaginella.

THE EDIBLE GARDEN

Starting an edible garden can be as simple or complicated as you like, from growing a handful of herbs in pots, to a few vegetables in polystyrene boxes or old car tyres, to the full commitment of a family-sized patch.

When you are starting off, the best approach is the KISS (keep it simple stupid!) technique. Enjoy just a few vegies or herbs until you get the hang of things. Once your confidence and your skills grow, extend the project. Rewarding first-timers include colourful sunflowers, sprouts and shoots, and easy leaf crops like spinach and silverbeet (Swiss chard).

Growing plants from seed is certainly the cheapest way to experiment. You can sow direct into the ground, or into seed-raising trays or individual pots. The back of the packet should advise you what method is best for your plants' needs.

FLOWER SALADS

More and more, salads today are using new ingredients to add colour and flavour. One of the 'new' additions happens to be one from bygone days ... flowers. Quite a number of flowers are edible, and not only look great but also taste terrific. Not just any old flowers, of course. Some can be highly poisonous, so it's best to stick to those you know are safe. Chives, rosemary, lavender, roses, violets, borage, cottage pinks (*Dianthus plumarius*), sage and rosella (*Hibiscus sabdariffa*) are perfectly okay. One common mistake, however, is to try using the larger-flowered garden marigold (*Tagetes* spp.) — which tastes terrible and, since it is used as an insect repellent, is probably bad for you as well — instead of the smaller-flowered pot marigold (*Calendula officinalis*), so be sure you've got the right one. Many of us can remember picking wild nasturtiums, a mass of orange, red and yellow flowers, choosing tender young leaves and blossoms to eat on tomato sandwiches. Their delicious peppery nuttiness was softened by the sweetness of the summer-ripe, juicy tomatoes.

Growing such a pretty salad is easy. You don't need a vegie patch; any patch of soil or container will do. Convert an old laundry tub into a living salad bowl, or plant up colanders with edibles and string them up like hanging baskets, cascading over with nasturtiums and other goodies.

SEEDS

GERMINATION

FLOWERS AND LEAVES

CLOCKWISE FROM TOP LEFT These are seeds picked from an existing clump of nasturtiums. Seeds are available in garden centres everywhere in a range of interesting perennial, easy-to-grow-at-home options such as corn salad, dandelion, radicchio, rocket, mizuna, baby spinach, cress and many more • Nasturtiums germinating in an egg carton. Sowing salad greens is easy. Egg cartons are great starter containers as they last long enough to germinate the seedlings and rot away completely after planting out • Harvesting flowers and leaves. The delicate flavours of freshly picked, home-grown produce cannot be compared with the bitterness of the older plants, and the convenience of having them on hand is another bonus • Pear blossoms and nasturtiums gathered in a tea towel. Flowers enliven fresh greens in a charming and unforgettable way.

GATHERED FLOWERS ON A TEATOWEL

FLOWER SALAD.

250 g (8 oz) mixed salad leaves,
   such as radicchio, frisée (endive),
   witlof (chicory), watercress,
   nasturtium leaves
handful herb sprigs, such as chervil,
   dill, fennel
45 g (1½ oz) edible flowers, such as
   nasturtium, borage, marigold
handful fresh croutons

DRESSING
3 tablespoons olive oil
2 tablespoons walnut oil
2 tablespoons wine vinegar
¼ teaasponn dijon mustard
salt and pepper to taste

Put the salad leaves, herb sprigs and edible flowers in a large serving bowl.
   To make the dressing, stir all the ingredients together in a small bowl or shake in a screw-top jar to combine.
   To serve, pour the dressing over the salad and toss lightly. Sprinke the croutons on top. Serves 4–6

YOU WILL NEED.

Seeds (see above)

Egg cartons work well as a biodegradable container for raising seedlings

Seed-raising mix

SPROUTS AND SHOOTS

The new growth of many plants makes a delicious, vitamin-packed edible salad green that is easily grown at home on the kitchen windowsill, ready for use and 'fresh from the garden'. Many seeds can be grown to eat as sprouts, but the most popular are beans, peas, radish, daikon, mung, onion and broccoli. Shoots are also easy to grow — things like mustard, cress and wheat. The most popular of all is alfalfa (lucerne sprouts), which contains all the essential amino acids and many vitamins. (Fully grown lucerne plants make excellent hay for cows and horses.)

YOU WILL NEED.

Cotton wool

Small dishes

Seeds

Scissors for harvesting

STEP 1

STEP 2

STEP 3

STEP 1   Sow seeds like wheat grass, cress and mustard directly onto moist cotton wool in small dishes.

STEP 2   Place dishes on a sunny windowsill and keep moist.

STEP 3   Harvest your shoots with sharp scissors as needed. You can store the cut shoots in the fridge for up to a week, but make sure to pat them dry first.

A spare 5 minutes.

SPROUTS IN A JAR

YOU WILL NEED: Glass jars; Muslin or old, clean stockings; String; Seeds

Simply put certified seed into a jar of tepid water and soak for 4 to 6 hours. Cover with a fine gauze-like material such as muslin or stockings, tie firmly, then drain by tipping upside down. Rinse daily with water and then drain. Harvesting can start in a few days.

Don't leave the sprouts too long before you harvest them —about 3–4 days after sprouting is ideal — because their quality and flavour quickly deteriorate. If you want to keep them longer, you're better off harvesting them, drying them off, then storing them in the fridge where they keep for a week. Only use a teaspoon or so at a time, so you can have small, continual harvests that you can eat fresh.

GROW YOUR OWN BABY SPINACH LEAVES

Baby spinach is one of those trendy vegetables that is ridiculously expensive to buy, expecially given the simplicity of growing it yourself. It can either be grown in pots or sown directly into the ground.

If you have sown your seeds directly into the ground, you will need to go back over the patch and remove the excess in a process called thinning out. This is especially important with root vegetables, such as carrots, which can grow with deformities if they are overcrowded below the surface.

This patch of spinach has come up after the seed was roughly broadcast direct into the soil, and without being thinned out will grow into a poor quality crop. The leaves of any seedlings discarded at this stage can be eaten fresh in a salad.

STEP 1

STEP 2

STEP 1   Use a stick or dibbler and pluck out any closely grouped seedlings.

STEP 2   These can be replanted in a less cluttered, more open space where other seedlings may have failed.

GARDENER'S TIP. It may sound obvious, but if you are growing your own herbs, don't be afraid to use them. The more you cut them back and thin them out, the healthier and tastier they'll be. Even if you're not eating them daily, they'll still need a trim to stay young, juicy and tender.

RAISING SUNFLOWERS

Sunflowers can be grown as potted plants, or sown into the garden direct (where in colder areas they will need protection from the frost until the weather is warmer).

Sow the seeds in individual containers and protect the growing seedlings until all chance of frosts has passed, then pot on into larger containers and place in a full-sun position, or plant them out. You can sow several seeds in the one container, but you will need to thin them down to one successful seedling per pot. The same technique is used for all frost-sensitive seedlings, such as tomatoes, eggplants (aubergines) and cucumbers.

STEP 1

STEP 2

STEP 1   Sow seeds singly, or 3 or 4 to a pot.

STEP 2   Label the pots. Place a protective cover over each pot, such as a cloche glasshouse, or keep them on a windowsill.

YOU WILL NEED.

Seeds

Pots

Seed-raising mix and, later, potting mix (compost)

Labels

Individual cloches (or make your own from cut-down plastic bottles)

HERB TOWER

Herbs and salad greens are a great thing to grow, especially if you can have them on hand whenever you need them. Potted herbs are fantastic for convenience, but if you want to grow more than a few types, things can become a bit cluttered at your back door.

Overcome this simply by placing herbs on a baker's stand so that they are arranged vertically or, better still, buy a three-tiered wire stand and plant straight into it — first lining it with sphagnum moss. The moss will not only stop the potting mix from slipping through the holes, it also has an extraordinary moisture-retaining ability, acting like a sponge to hold water and save you being a slave to the garden. The high levels of zinc that occur naturally in the sphagnum moss will also keep your herbs' roots healthy.

Your three-course meal awaits you, without occupying too much space, and it looks fabulous.

STEP 1   STEP 2   STEP 3

YOU will need.

10-litre (10½ qt) bag sphagnum moss

30-litre (31½ qt) bag of potting mix (compost) specially formulated for herbs

Wire tower or stand. Look out in bric-a-brac stores and antique auctions for genuine Victorian items

About 50 small herbs (10 cm/4 in pots are ideal)

STEP 1   Working from the top tier down, line the base and sides of the stand with sphagnum moss, then a handful of potting mix (compost). Not all herbs are perennials. Some, like basil, die off over winter, so planting these at the top will mean it's easy to replace them each season. You can add snow peas (mangetout), another annual, around the perimeter so that they can trail down and twine around the stand.

STEP 2   Next, plant the second tier. Here cascading herbs, such as prostrate rosemary, are placed around the edges so that they can trail easily. This level contains a mixture of salad greens, including the purple-foliaged Asian mustard, and rocket (arugula), popular in Italian cuisine.

STEP 3   Complete the last layer with more herbs. As this level won't receive as much sun (due to the tiers above shading it), use more shade-tolerant plants such as perpetual lettuce, French parsley (chervil) and mint. Here, peppermint is planted on its side to form a living wall of fragrant leaves.

GARDEN VENTURES

These are creative projects that you can really get stuck into, and which will reward you with many years of beauty. Some projects comprise two parts. For example, making a tripod for clematis requires an hour in the garden in itself, while planting the climber and tying it on constitutes another task.

Use these projects as a guide, and experiment with your own innovations … the double-layered pot would be just as lovely planted with another fruiting or fragrant plant, and the moss and fern ball basket can work with annuals, or edibles like strawberries to make a mobile brunch basket.

MAKING A MOSS AND FERN BASKET

A hanging basket filled with an assortment of lush ferns and moss makes a cooling oasis for the verandah or balcony. Imagine your basket as a globe of the world, and plan to have ferns sprouting out of each continent, not forgetting Antarctica. This is an upside-down basket you'll enjoy looking at from all angles.

YOU WILL NEED.

A prefabricated sphagnum moss liner in matching size (they vary)

Atomizer

Pliers

A hanging basket

Premium standard potting mix (compost)

An assortment of ferns such as hare's foot, bird's nest, brake and rough maidenhair (mix textures and colours for added interest)

Moss such as bush and sphagnum moss

STEP 1

STEP 2

STEP 3

STEP 1   Put the moss liner in the basket and moisten using an atomizer or a light hosing (set the nozzle to a fine spray). To make planting easier, use the pliers to detach one of the three chains from the ring at the top of the basket. (When the basket is finished, reattach the chain for hanging.)

STEP 2   Puncture a number of holes in the sides and towards the base of the liner. Keep the holes small enough to hold the rootballs of the ferns snugly, so they won't fall out when the basket is hung.

STEP 3   Start at the base of the basket with one of the smallest ferns. Holding the fronds gently in one hand, carefully thread them through a hole to the outside (the roots should always be inside the basket). Alternatively, wrap the fronds in a tube of newspaper or similar to thread them through the hole. Add some potting mix (compost) around the rootball. Repeat, placing the smallest ferns near the base and the next smallest up the sides. Add potting mix as necessary to fill up any air pockets.

STEP 4   Plant your feature ferns, such as bird's nest and hare's foot ferns, in the top of the basket, then add enough potting mix to make a mound to complete your globe. Fill any gaps between the ferns with pieces of moss. Lastly, water well.

STEP 4

GARdeNeR's TiP.   To prevent drying out, hang your fern basket on the shady side of the house (normally the south side in the southern hemisphere, the north side in the northern hemisphere). Use the moss as mulch to keep the soil and roots moist. Water regularly using a hose fitted with a soft watering rose or water breaker.

DOUBLE-LAYERED POT

Sometimes the most ordinary things can be transformed with a little special treatment, like a beautifully wrapped present. To give your pot plants a little lift, try underplanting them with a complementary annual, cascading groundcover or tufted grass.

This can be done very simply by creating holes for new plants in existing large tubs, but can also look fabulous when a double-layered effect is created using two pots, one inside the other. This gives two advantages: the central pot can be lifted above the base pot, adding height, and the 'under' plants have their own potting mix and don't have to compete with the roots from the centrepiece.

Cumquats are often grown in pots, but can look a little boring when not in fruit or flower. The two-layer treatment works well with this young 'Nagumi', the tear-drop cumquat.

STEP 1

STEP 2

STEP 3

YOU WiLL Need.

Premium potting mix (compost) (containing water-storing crystals and slow-release fertilizer)

Two pots of similar style, one at least 10 cm (4 in) larger across than the other to allow the smaller pot to sit comfortably inside it

A central feature plant; here we have used a cumquat

A dozen or so seedlings to form the base ring; here we have used mondo grass (*Ophiopogon*)

STEP 1   The feature plant is potted into a squat terracotta pot, in this case about 25 cm (10 in) across. Place a base layer of potting mix (compost) inside the larger pot, which is about 35 cm (14 in) across. This forms the platform on which your centre pot sits. Make sure the potting mix is level so that the overall effect will be even, not lopsided. If necessary, you can use an upturned pot as a plinth instead. This is particularly useful for larger tubs.

STEP 2   Choose small plants to fill the space between the two pots, or use plants that can be broken up into smaller segments without harm. Mondo grass (*Ophiopogon*) is ideal because it separates so easily, but lobelia, blue fescue grass or trailing ivy-leaf geraniums can also work well, depending on the look you're after.

STEP 3   Fill the void with potting mix. Plant the seedlings to form an even ring around the centre plant, then backfill around their roots. Water well to help remove any air pockets and settle your new plants into their two-storey home!

CLEMATIS TRIPOD

Rustic, homemade frames are a charming way to support your favourite climber. In this example, a wild garden needed some vertical element, and a simple tripod with a colourful clematis was an easy solution.

Make sure you choose green stems for your support, as they will be more subtle and pliable. This support is made from fruit tree branches and elm twigs, but any flexible wood will be okay.

Don't limit yourself to just one tripod — a few supported climbing vegies would be lovely in a potager — or adapt a tripod to make a unique Christmas tree. Fill the inside with presents, tie on the decorations, place in a decorative glazed pot and you will have something that creates quite an impact.

YOU WILL NEED.

Secateurs (garden shears)

A tree you can cut lengths from (peach blossom and Chinese elm are used here), or purchase willow wands from your florist supplier

Florists' wire or twine for tying

A clematis (or similar climber)

STEP 1

STEP 2

STEP 1   Cut branches about 1.8 m (6 ft) long and 2 cm (¾ in) in diameter from a suitable tree.

STEP 2   Prepare seven 1.8 m (6 ft) lengths by removing side branches with secateurs. Save the longer clippings (roughly 30 cm/12 in or so) for the spiral.

GARDENER'S TIP.   Clematis should be planted with one node below soil level. This helps them sucker and shoot from the base.

STEP 3

STEP 4

STEP 5

STEP 6

STEP 7

STEP 8

STEP 3   Run your hands along the side branches, which will be used as the horizontals, to remove small leaves.

STEP 4   Set the smaller lengths to soak in a large bucket of water, curving them against the side, which will not only help keep them pliable, but also start shaping them.

STEP 5   Place the 1.8 m (6 ft) lengths in a circle, evenly spaced, and the tie tops together like a teepee with florists' wire or twine.

STEP 6   Starting about 30 cm (12 in) up from the base, wind a number of 30 cm (12 in) lengths in and out of the teepee supports until you've made a complete circle. Wire or tie them to the supports and to each other if necessary to secure as you go.

STEP 7   Add more branches to your circle till it has sufficient strength. Stagger the ends so that the twigs stop and start at random intervals.

STEP 8   Repeat steps 3 and 4 until you have another three circles, much like the hoops on an old-fashioned petticoat.

STEP 9

STEP 10

STEP 11

STEP 9   Position your frame in its final resting place and plant the clematis 5 cm (2 in) below its existing soil level, so that it is buried slightly. This will encourage it to shoot up vigorously from the base.

STEP 10   Tie tendrils onto the frame.

STEP 11   Mulch and water well.

A spare 5 minutes.

Mowing the grass every weekend will hardly be a chore with this size patch, proving that size does matter!

Some ornamental grasses are small enough to use as a microgarden, your own tiny plot of turf to remind yourself of greener pastures. Buy a punnet of small tough sedges and plant them into a stylish trough, using their wonderful leaves to brighten up a table top.

This dwarf carex loves a wet spot, so it is one of the few plants that happily grows in water (see page 32). It will also succeed with a saucer beneath its pot, which makes it ideal for tabletops. The simplicity of green, black and white is very restful.

For a variation on the theme, why not sow yourself a tray of wheat grass or lawn seed, and trim it off to form a neatly clipped lawn?

TAKEN TO TASK

TIPS FOR SUCCESSFUL
GARDEN MAINTENANCE

RECYCLING

Gardeners should pride themselves on being some of the 'greenest' people around, and not just in regard to their thumbs either! Smart gardeners use their heads, recycling as much organic matter back into the garden as possible. This is not only good for the global environment; it is also good for the garden. Lawn clippings, vegie matter, fallen leaves and paper products can all be turned into compost, which is the best fertilizer known for plants and works as a wonderful soil conditioner and plant tonic. Fallen leaves and branches can be made into mulch, and worms can busily consume your kitchen scraps and create a fantastic liquid fertilizer.

WORM FARM

Most of us don't like the idea of throwing anything away. The 'reuse, recycle and refuse' mantra is being chanted everywhere. Yet many householders happily sort out the plastic bottles, paper and tins from their garbage and overlook what is perhaps the gardener's greatest resource ... their vegetable scraps.

While the idea of a compost heap may not appeal to you, or you may simply not have the space — a worm farm is the simplest and most compact method of recycling available. Worms have been doing it for aeons, so they know what to do — all you need to do is provide them with food and a shady place to shelter. After they've finished their hard work digesting your scraps, you're left with a nutrient-rich compost (known as castings) and a soluble fertilizer, perfect for giving your garden and pots a boost.

Worm compost and fertilizer are odour free, so they can be used on indoor plants too.

YOU WILL NEED.

5-litre (5¼ qt) bag of peat moss

Compost worms

Ready-made worm farm

Plastic sheeting

Fruit and vegetable scraps

Scissors

STEP 1

STEP 2

STEP 3

STEP 1   Line the working box of the worm farm (the top one with perforations in it) with dampened newspaper. This will rot down quickly, but it stops the worms' bedding material from slipping through the holes in the set-up stage. Next, add some moistened peat moss to cover the base of the box to a depth of about 5 cm (2 in). This will be the worms' 'bed'.

STEP 2   Add a box of fresh worms. Worms will stop breeding once they reach the maximum amount for the worm farm, and you can start your farm off slowly with 500 worms, or give it a revved-up start by buying 4000. Make sure that the worms haven't been sealed in plastic takeaway containers; if this has happened, they will have been deprived of air and may die.

STEP 3   Add foods like tea leaves and fruit or vegetable scraps, even coffee grounds, but never add meat, dairy or bread as they may attract vermin. Worms love it if the scraps are small and partially decomposed, so try to keep the scraps in a sealed container (like an ice-cream bucket) for a few days before adding them to your worm farm. You can also give them small amounts of soaked cardboard cartons and vacuum cleaner dust — worms really are the ultimate re-users!

STEP 4

STEP 4   Cover the scraps with moistened cardboard, hessian or a sheet of plastic, and close the lid. In a couple of weeks you will be able to collect the castings from the middle box and the liquid manure that accumulates in the lowest box to use on your garden.

GARDENER'S TIP. Some organic matter, such as onions, citrus peel and tomatoes, is quite acidic and can be harmful to the worms. These should only be added sparingly.

HANDY HINT.
If you don't want to go to the expense of buying a ready-made worm farm, you can construct one very cheaply from three polystyrene foam boxes stacked one on top of the other.

MULCHING

The quickest and cheapest way to transform your garden is to mulch it. This instant facelift not only covers a multitude of sins, it's also great for the garden and your plants' health. Fresh mulch can be picked up for next to nothing from your local authority, or you can contact a tree lopper or arborist who works in your area — they are often happy to supply a truckload at a very reasonable price.

Mulch provides a blanket layer over your soil. Normally about 10 cm (4 in) thick, it regulates soil temperature by keeping roots cool in summer and warm in winter. Depending on the time of year in which you mulch, you can influence soil temperature. For example, if you mulch at the end of autumn, you will keep the soil warmer for longer, while mulching in early spring will keep the soil cooler longer and prevent heat being trapped in summer. Mulching conserves moisture and cuts down on watering requirements by reducing evaporation from the soil surface and increasing water penetration, and controls weeds by preventing weed seeds from germinating.

HANDY HINT.

Never mulch up to the collar or trunk of a plant as this can cause both collar rot and ringbarking.

Mulches are available in many forms, both organic and inorganic. Organic mulches include leaf mulch, pine bark, red gum chips, lucerne, straw, newspaper, compost, rice husks and sugar cane. An effective mulch should not be dislodged by wind and rain and should have a loose enough structure to allow water to soak through easily.

Some mulches — for example, lucerne, compost and sugar cane — have a high nitrogen content. These mulches improve the soil fertility, but they rot down quickly and so need to be replaced every few months. Never use peat moss as a mulch as it repels water once it is dry; rather, blend it into the soil and use it as a soil conditioner.

Inorganic mulches — such as black plastic, weed control mat, scoria and decorative gravels — are not really 'garden friendly'. They add nothing to the soil structure, and once these mulches are in place, soil additives are difficult to incorporate. They tend to raise the soil temperature and some can even stop your soil from breathing, which can lead to serious problems. Use them sparingly in the garden: pebbles look great as top dressings for feature pots but can be a pain to maintain in larger areas. Plastics work well under gravel paths and other places where you have no intention of planting.

STEP 1

STEP 2

STEP 3

STEP 1   For the mulch to work effectively in suppressing weeds, you'll first need to remove the weeds by hand (see page 102) or with weedicide (see pages 106–7). Don't be tempted just to cover them up as they will soon reappear.

STEP 2   Mulch is light, so you will easily be able to wheel it by the barrow load to its destination.

STEP 3   Tip the barrow, spreading some of the mulch out as you go.

STEP 4   Spread it out over the soil using a leaf rake, keeping the overall depth to about 10 cm (4 in).

STEP 4

COMPOST TUBE

For some people, building a compost heap is just too big a job. For others, there is simply not the space needed to do it. Worm farms and compost tubes are ideal ways to dispose of fruit and vegie scraps thoughtfully, without much effort being involved. One compost tube is enough for the average household. Just move it about the garden every few months so it can nourish a different area.

Because there are holes in the base, garden worms can enter the tube. They will help break down the scraps and take the nutrients into the soil.

YOU WILL NEED.

15-litre (15¾ qt) plastic bucket

Drill and hole-saw bit

Compost scraps

Worms (optional)

STEP 1

STEP 2

STEP 3

STEP 4

STEP 1   Using a 3 cm (1½ in) hole-saw bit on your drill (or a spade bit the same size), cut a number of evenly spaced holes around the sides and in the base of your bucket.

STEP 2   Partially bury the bucket in a handy yet unobtrusive position in the garden, with the lid on top. The holes provide aeration, and access for worms.

STEP 3   Tip in all the household vegetable scraps and fruit peelings you've collected over the last couple of days.

STEP 4   Close the lid and add scraps as they accumulate.

GARDENER'S TIP. Adding a handful of soil and some compost worms will help kick-start the decomposition process.

PLANT RENEWAL

The secret to stimulating new growth on plants is something that gardeners have always been keen to unravel. Nothing slows down a plant more than it being tired of it's position, having used up all the nutrients in the soil, needing to be divided up and replanted or having outgrown its pot and needing to go up a size.

Some plants need a pick-me-up with pruning. The type of pruning required depends on each plant's individual needs. Many shrubs are improved greatly by frequent small prunings, called tip pruning — each time a new shoot is removed, two grow in its place. With tip pruning leggy plants are transformed by regular trimming, hedges are thickened and new growth is stimulated. Flowers require their own type of pruning with the removal of old blooms, a technique known as deadheading.

Removing the excess growth of climbers is a year-round task. The tactics needed to keep them under control vary, depending on what sort of climber you are talking about. Evergreens, are best trimmed back hard after flowering, then kept in check with regular removal of wayward tendrils throughout their growing season; some climbers, such as self-clinging figs and ivy, need trimming where you don't wish them to grow to keep them from marking paintwork or stonework permanently; while deciduous climbers, like ornamental grape vines and wisteria, are best trimmed in winter.

REPOTTING

Repotting can be necessary for a number of reasons, the most frequent being that your plant has outgrown its pot, and simply needs to go up a size or two to be able to continue growing healthily. This is indicated in a number of ways: your plant wilts quickly between drinks, roots are showing on the surface, and it has yellowing leaves.

STEP 1

STEP 2

STEP 3

STEP 4

STEP 5

STEP 6

STEP 7

STEP 8

STEP 1   For a closer look, upturn the pot and prise out the rootball. Plants showing the symptoms described on the previous page will either be rootbound, with a mass of roots and no room for any potting mix, or have roots that have started to twist and spiral, turning in on themselves and tying themselves in knots.

STEP 2   Where this has happened it is important to unravel the roots and cut off any irretrievably tangled conglomerates of root and repot into a larger container (or, in the case of bonsai, back into the same container with fresh bonsai mix).

STEP 3   Line the base of the pot with premium standard mix (compost). Crocking the base (putting broken pieces of pot or gravel at the bottom) can be dispensed with, unless the drainage hole is so large that the mix runs straight through. Always use the best potting mix you can get your hands on (or into!).

STEP 4   Add some water-storing crystals if you live in a drought-prone climate. These will swell up and act as reservoirs, like sponges, for a less-than-rainy day.

STEP 5   Add enough potting mix to bring the plant to the right finished level so you won't have to build up soil around its neck, and backfill with more mix.

STEP 6   Using your hands, tamp down the potting mix lightly. Never ram the mix down hard as this eliminates all the air, which is as important for root growth as any other element in the mix.

STEP 7   At this point it is wise to use a gentle root tonic, such as seaweed solution, to water your plant in. This stimulates root growth, and will ensure that your repotted plant settles into its new home quickly.

STEP 8   Mulch with whatever material you find attractive to dress up your pot. Here, fine bluish gravel has been used.

A spare 5 minutes.

PAINTING POTS

If you're tired of one look, consider painting your pots. This grey cement pot is being transformed quickly and simply with off-white paint.

DIVIDING

The garden is often relegated to the very end of any building project or renovation, with people generally prioritizing expenditure on carpets and furniture over paving, lawn and shrubbery. This doesn't mean you need be stuck with a dustbowl for a backyard. Luckily, plants are programmed to reproduce, and tapping into the many ways they can do it is an easy way to get a garden for very little cost.

PLANTS FOR FREE

The cheapest way of filling empty spaces is by division of plants that may already be in your garden. This way you instantly obtain a reasonable sized plant with its own root system ready to go. And often keen gardening friends will come to the party. Many perennial plants are multiplied this way, including asters, shasta daisies and chrysanthemums, arum lilies, carex, agapanthus, cannas, kangaroo paws, cliveas, cast iron plants (*Aspidistra elatior*), and many more. These plants form clumps which can be divided up into several separate plants, and indeed benefit from being broken up.

It is simply a matter of splitting up an established clump or pot. Using a spade for something like agapanthus, a trowel for the *Tradescantia* cultivar shown here, cut the clump into sections. Remove any damaged leaves and trim any broken roots. Plant the new sections directly into the garden bed and water in well. This is normally a job for late winter or early spring, just before new growth commences and while the roots are still dormant, to cause the plants minimum stress by the disturbance.

AS EASY AS 1 – 2 – 3

You can also save money by buying just a few potted plants that you can divide. Your new garden might look a little sparse, but the plants quickly grow and get up to speed, and you'll have many more plants as a result. Here a 15 cm (6¼ in) pot of the pretty green-and-purple leaved *Tradescantia*, commonly known as rhoeo, has been broken up into a dozen or so smaller plants to make a border.

STEP 1

STEP 2

STEP 3

STEP 1   Using your hands or a trowel, break the plant into two or three large pieces.

STEP 2   Using your fingers, gently separate the plant into individual sections, each with roots and leaves.

STEP 3   Plant the divisions into the ground and water in well.

CLIPPING HEDGES

Planting a hedge means committing yourself to a regular maintenance regime of pruning, gathering and discarding clippings, and replenishing exhausted soil with fertilizer, but the results are spectacular and well worth the effort. Nothing beats a formal hedge to give classic elegance to a garden, or an informal hedge to provide an instant screen from neighbours or to block unsightly views. The reward for your labours is a serene garden room with privacy.

YOU WILL NEED.

Long-bladed trimmers

Ladder

Leaf rake

String line (mason's line),
if required

The tricks to maintaining a healthy hedge are simple: first, make sure as much of your hedge as possible gets access to the sun's rays; second, trim little and often to reduce stress and encourage side-branching and bushiness from the base — this means not leaving things to the last minute (in other words, pruning should start virtually at planting time and be done regularly from that day on); and third, use the right equipment.

STEP 1

STEP 2

STEP 3

STEP 4

S T E P   1   To keep your hedge growing evenly all over, try to ensure your pruning doesn't create any shadowed areas. Size doesn't matter but shape does. Tapering the sides inwards is the best way of allowing the sun to shine over all the plants, especially if any are struggling due to their aspect.

S T E P   2   Tip pruning forces dormant buds to break into leaf, which then creates a bushier, denser hedge. You can trim anything from a small strip to lengths of about 20 cm (8 in). This will help your hedge to stay vigorous and problem free. Make sure your equipment is sharp and clean. Long-bladed trimmers are perfect for thin branches (as on this pittosporum) and parrot-beaked secateurs (garden shears) for slightly thicker branches. If you need to strain as you prune, then either your equipment is blunt or you need to go up a size to, say, loppers for thicker branches.

S T E P   3   A ladder is often necessary to reach the top of a tall hedge — use a stable, well-cared for ladder for the job as you don't want to fall, especially with sharp things in your hands.

S T E P   4   A leaf rake is particularly useful, not only for clean-up but also for brushing trapped clippings out of your hedge. You can use a string line (mason's line) to get a hedge straight, but a good eye is just as effective and much easier!

CORDYLINE MAINTENANCE

Many plants develop a straggle of dead foliage as they grow taller. Some are self-cleaning and shed their old foliage naturally as they grow, but others that don't shed need a helping hand to look their best. Many palms fall into the latter category. The extremely fashionable cordyline, or cabbage tree palm, is one which needs occasional attention to keep it looking good. All you have to do is strip the lower leaves by hand as they die off. Others, such as the coin-spotted tree fern and the bangalow palm, do this themselves ... but you'll still find their waste at their base!

STEP 1   Assess how much of the damaged outer foliage of the cordyline needs to be removed, then gently pull off affected leaves.

STEP 2   Collect the leaves and put them in the compost.

STEP 1

STEP 2

A spare 5 minutes.

CROWN LIFTING

Many trees naturally shoot branches from low down the trunk. This may be just the look you're after, but in most gardens you will need access under the canopy, so you will need to lift the crown.

To encourage a tree with a single trunk and plenty of head room, cleanly remove any side shoots as they appear on the trunk. Then remove lower branches with secateurs (garden shears) (or a pruning saw for thick limbs), but leave the ridge collar (the skin-like fold of bark at the branch junction) intact as a small stub to reduce the chance of bacterial infection entering the tree. Trees naturally compartmentalize at these junctions to protect themselves, and you should respect this when pruning. Any shoots that develop on the cleaned trunk can be rubbed off as they swell, which is by far the least disruptive way to tackle undergrowth.

MAPLE MAINTENANCE

Japanese maples, especially the grafted weeping types, in marginal climates are prone to developing deadwood. Spring is the perfect time to check over your plants, as it is easy to spot any dead wood that has not shot into leaf. Saw off any branches that have died, neatly and cleanly, flush with the adjoining branch or even the trunk. Trim off twiggy dead wood with secateurs (garden shears) or simply break it off with your finger tips. Take the opportunity to mulch your maple with rotted down cow manure, then watch for aphids as the new leaves appear, as they are particularly susceptible to attack. Get rid of any free-loaders with chilli soap spray (see page 113).

REMOVE DEAD WOOD WITH A SAW

YOU WILL NEED.

Pruning saw

Secateurs (garden shears)

Cow manure

A SPARE 5 MINUTES.

PRUNING FERNS

Tree ferns form their trunk by putting on new fronds each season. The trick to maintaining a healthy looking plant is to remove old fronds as they wither. Some varieties, like the coin spotted tree fern, drop their fronds cleanly by themselves; however, others will need a tidy up. Either cut off neatly with a saw, or just break the frond away with your hands.

Some tree ferns, like *Dicksonia Antartica* are remarkable in that you can cut their trunk in two and replant the top part, which will continue growing – a useful trick if it has outgrown its spot – though make sure you don't do this on the *Cyathea* varieties (see right) as they will die.

SHARPENING SECATEURS

With regular pruning a key to keeping your plants healthy, you'll need to keep your equipment in top shape. Keeping your secateurs (garden shears) sharp is an easy job, perfect for a winter's day when the garden is calling you but it's too cold to contemplate spending time outside, or for any other spare moment. The difference sharpening your secateurs makes to their performance always makes me wonder why I took so long to get around to it!

YOU will need.

General-purpose lubricant

'Thin' free-flowing oil (I use sewing machine oil)

Screwdriver

Sharpening stone

Soft cloth

STEP 1

STEP 2

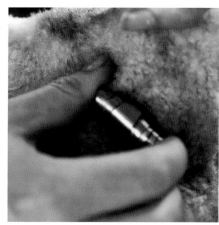

STEP 3

STEP 4

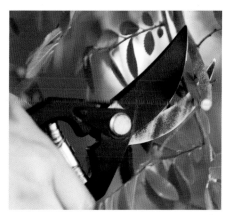

STEP 5

STEP 1 Undo your secateurs (garden shears). Each brand is different, but they should all come apart using either a screwdriver (or coin) to undo the screw, and a small shifter or sometimes an allen key to loosen the main bolt. General-purpose lubricant can also help!

STEP 2 Lay out all the parts and use general-purpose lubricant to lightly oil the blades, spring and other mechanisms.

STEP 3 Rub the parts down carefully with a soft cloth to remove dirt and rust.

STEP 4 Using a sharpening stone and a little free-flowing 'thin' oil, carefully sharpen the cutting blade, working with the angle on the angled side of the blade, then rubbing the flat back of the blade against the stone to remove possible burrs. The other blade should remain blunt in bypass secateurs, or flat in parrot-beaked secateurs. Wax the handles if they are wooden.

STEP 5 Reassemble the secateurs and tighten so that the blades are held in position firmly, but still slide easily against each other. Wipe off any excess oil. Now test them — the new edge should give a beautifully clean cut.

GARDENER'S TIP. When you are using parot-beaked secateurs to trim small branches back to the trunk of a tree or to the main stems of a shrub, put the cutting blade against the trunk to ensure the cleanest cut, as shown in the picture on page 78.

PRUNING CREEPING FIG

Some climbers are particularly unique in that they are self-clinging, that is, they don't require staking, trellis or support in any way, as they have aerial roots which stick onto any surface — even glass. Creeping fig (*Ficus pumila*) and ivy are the two most commonly seen self-clingers, but others include Boston ivy (also known as Virginia creeper) and euonymus. Creeping fig is perhaps the best of all, with its small dainty leaves, which are the juvenile foliage of the plant. The trick is to keep it well pruned. Outward growth can mature into the adult form, which is large and aggressive and not nearly so attractive. Stray growth can cause unsightly damage. Wear gloves for clean-up as the white, milky sap is sticky and can cause skin irritation.

STEP 1 STEP 2

YOU WILL NEED.

Flat-bladed shears

Gloves for clean-up

Razor blade for removing bits of aerial roots stuck to walls

STEP 1 Peel back any unwanted growth.

STEP 2 Using flat-bladed shears, cut away excess growth.

STEP 3 Again using the flat shears, trim off any outward-growing leaders.

GARDENER'S TIP.
This is a job that needs to be done regularly, otherwise the fig's roots will leave tracks where you don't want them, especially on painted surfaces. Some cultivars, like the variegated 'Frosty' and the smaller-leaved 'Minima', can revert to the parent form in places, so trim these bits off too. Razor blades should get rid of the tracks.

PRUNING GRAPE VINES

Grape vines can be either ornamental or fruiting. Ornamental grape vines are fabulous cultivated over a pergola, offering beautiful autumn-toned leaves and cool summer shade. Fruiting vines, of course, provide an abundance of luscious fruit. For ornamental grapes, the key pruning lesson is to remove bulky growth. For fruiting vines the maintenance of a single stem (like a trunk) from which the main branches extend along the wires of a trellis requires a more elaborate technique — four main 'arms' are kept to grow as horizontals, and these have a few short stumpy 'fingers' from which the new fruiting growth shoots.

YOU WILL NEED.

Flat-bladed shears

Secateurs (garden shears)

Ladder

HANDY HINT.

For best autumn colour, choose a named ornamental grape vine like 'Alicante Bouchet'.

STEP 1

STEP 2

STEP 3

STEP 1   A summer jungle of vine in dire need of pruning back — but leave it until winter.

STEP 2   You can cut the excess tendrils and leaders back quite savagely, leaving a rather knotty skeleton. Not terribly attractive, perhaps, but it won't be like this for long ...

STEP 3   Collect the waste, but only put it in the compost heap after it's been through a shredder. You can also use it for kindling once it's dried out a little.

HANDY HINT.

Instead of putting out green waste for the local authority collection, consider buying a mulcher so you can convert prunings into mulch.

A SPARE 5 MINUTES.

CLEARING GUTTERS

Take five, every few months, to check your eaves and gutters for encroaching growth from climbers. They can quickly grow up into your roof and start to cause damage to the building, so be vigilant. This Rangoon creeper (*Quisqualis indica*) is known for its fabulous flower, but needs to be tempered in its strong growth so it won't swallow up your roof!

PRUNING WISTERIA

WINTER PRUNING

You need to pay special attention when pruning wisteria in winter (see left). The key issue is to watch out for, and keep, the flowering spurs. You can tell the difference between flower and leaf buds through close inspection. Flower buds have a fine fur or down on them and are quite close together, while leaf buds are further apart and have no down. Clipping away the non-flowering growth will just remove excess growth, and ensure masses of spring blooms.

SUMMER PRUNING

After your wisteria has flowered in spring, it is extremely important to keep its subsequent wildly enthusiastic tendril growth under control (see below). Wisteria has been known to break iron bars, so timber pergola slats are no challenge at all.

STEP 1

STEP 2

STEP 3

STEP 1   Locate the long, string-like tendrils.

STEP 2   Trim back to the main woody framework.

STEP 3   Continue cutting back excess tendril growth until only a fraction of the summer growth remains.

YOU WILL NEED.

Flat-bladed shears

Secateurs (garden shears)

Ladder

GARDENER'S TIP. There are many varieties of wisteria.
Ensure you get the cultivar you want by buying only cutting-grown, labelled stock. The double variety shown on the right is *Wisteria sinensis* 'Floraplena'.

PRUNING ROSES

A good deal of mystery and confusion shrouds rose pruning, most of it spouted by self-important 'experts', which can leave the average rose owner a little afraid of tackling what is really an enormously hardy plant. While there are some roses, like climbers and weepers, that need special attention, most are foolproof. When you think that roses in the growing nurseries are pruned mechanically straight across the top, and that in the olden days they used to be burned to the ground (done to promote new growth when roses weren't grafted onto a different understock), you realize that there is not much that these guys can't take!

The most commonsense advice is to prune your roses three times a year — once in winter, again when you cut the flowers for an arrangement, and once more when you walk past them and deadhead their fading blooms. The most commonly discussed pruning is that in winter, but the other cuts are just as important for ongoing flowering and healthy growth.

Clean up as you prune, removing the prickly stems so you won't accidentally come across them in the garden barefoot or gloveless. Always clean your secateurs between pruning individual plants to stop disease spreading, dipping them in either antiseptic or bleach.

YOU will need.

Secateurs

Pruning saw

Gloves

Sturdy, closed-in shoes

Long sleeves

STEP 1

STEP 2

WINTER PRUNING

The winter prune involves cutting roses back to what is called an open vase shape. This should result in three or four main branches of good vigour which don't cross over each other, and thus allow as much light into the plant as possible — this means you get more flowers and fewer fungal problems.

Cut each branch on the diagonal and prune to an outward-facing bud so that the new growth does not crowd the centre of the bush.

STEP 1   A pruning saw can be used to remove very old, trunk-like shoots that are no longer productive. The bark on these has usually changed to a greyish colour.

STEP 2   Remaining shoots need to have one-half to two-thirds of their growth removed. Cut on the diagonal to just above an outward-facing bud.

A SPARE 5 MINUTES.

DEADHEADING

Flowering is the beginning of a plant's reproductive cycle, while the setting of seeds represents its end. If you interfere with this process by taking off the old flowers before they get a chance to set seed, you will trick the plant into flowering again. This is known as deadheading and it is an easy 5-minute job that will ensure your garden gets a second flush of flowers. Simply nip the fading blooms off just above the next leaf shoot, and wait for the show to begin all over again.

Deadheading roses can mean either just nipping off the old blooms to stop them from forming hips, or removing them with a long stem as if you were cutting them for a vase.

LAWN CARE

Wherever you have grass, maintenance is inevitable. The amount of time you spend on your lawn will depend on the type of surface you are trying to achieve. Obviously a croquet lawn or bowling green will need loads of work, with greens mown every day during the summer months. For a less fastidious finish, in a backyard where children and dogs run riot, a weekly cut in spring and summer, and a monthly cut in the cooler months is plenty.

Other maintenance jobs, such as keeping your lawn regularly aerated, fed and watered once a week, will ensure that the grass stays sturdy and green, an ideal foil for flower-filled garden beds or a hard-wearing play area for children.

MOWING LAWNS

You need to consider what type of mower will be best suited to your needs. Small backyards may suit a push mower or small electric mower, while larger lawns may warrant a ride-on mower. But be mindful of the manoeuvrability of your mower as you may have issues if you have lots of garden beds — you could actually be better off with a decent rotary mower.

CYLINDER MOWER

HAND MOWER

ROTARY MOWER

CYLINDER MOWERS

These fabulous cutting machines really are the Rolls-Royce of mowers. For a professional 'bowling green' lawn they are hard to beat. Use a string line (mason's line) to establish the first run. Pegging out a guide like this will make all the difference to your finished product. The following runs just need to follow the cut line as the guide.

HAND MOWERS

For small areas, the old-fashioned cylinder hand mower works beautifully. They have the same cutting action as the fuel-powered versions, but unfortunately rely on brute strength to work. The trick is never to let your grass get too tall, as it's a hard slog going through anything longer than a few centimetres. Another one of its downsides is a lack of flexibility in cutting height.

VICTA! THE FIRST ROTARY MOWER

This fine Australian invention, developed in the 1950s by Mervyn Victor Richardson for his son's mowing run, was at first a lightweight machine-powered cylinder mower. So popular was it that the mower went on to become a huge business in its own right.

The final design had a rotary cutting action, now seen in the many brands of mower bought for average garden grass-cutting purposes. Ride-on mowers, with the same rotary action, are fantastic for small acreage and large stretches of open lawn. They lack the manoeuvrability of smaller mowers, however, and you still need a small mower or a brush cutter (string trimmer) for any tricky bits (such as curves and around tree).

EDGING LAWNS

HANDY HINT.

Raising the level of your garden bed with brick, stone or timber retainers not only defines the edge but can also improve drainage and give you a cutting edge.

The mower will never be enough for maintaining a lawn. Edgers, brush cutters (string trimmers), secateurs (garden shears) and also half-moon spades are necessary tools of the trade for producing a finished look.

Despite your best efforts, the vigorous nature of grass means that it will always be finding its way into areas where you don't want it. Various forms of garden edging, from flexible timber mowing strips to plastic edging, will help control the problem, but you will inevitably have to 'do the edges' from time to time.

Keeping garden bed layout simple, with gently curving or straight lines, and making sure that any edging you put in goes down at least 10 cm (4 in) into the ground to halt the progress of underground rhizomes, will all help make the best of the situation.

STEP 1

STEP 2

STEP 3

S T E P 1   Grass grows with runners, which inevitably find their way into garden beds, across driveways and up garden walls or tree trunks, and needs to be controlled.

S T E P 2   Clipping small areas by hand (against rockery edges, for example) is probably the easiest way of going about things, and definitely the safest way of keeping grass away from tree trunks.

S T E P 3   If you find using a brush cutter is easier, put guards around tree trunks to prevent ringbarking them.

S T E P 4   You can use chicken wire, but the plastic trellis mesh shown here is much easier on the hands, and can easily be moved from tree to tree as you work.

STEP 4

GARdeNeR's Tips.

Grass trimmings and clippings can be turned into compost. Gather up waste and put into the compost as you go.

By wielding a rake with gusto, you will remove some of the thatch (dead grass build-up), which will help water penetrate and encourage healthier growth.

BARE PATCHES

Fixing bare patches in a lawn is easy in warm weather. Many grasses grow from runners, including the popular couch, kikuyu and buffalo grass. If you have bare patches caused by excessive wear and tear or neglect, spring and summer are the times to fix it – and the solution is cheap and simple. This is a technique that can be used not only to repair bare patches, but also to plant an entire lawn, provided you can source enough runners. Just transplant or encourage runners into the bare patches, cover over with washed river sand, keep pets and foot-traffic off — and wait a few weeks.

STEP 1

STEP 2

STEP 3

STEP 1   Locate a healthy section of your lawn. There you'll find many runners that you can tease up off the turf bed. Dig some of these up, or even pull them up by hand. Shake off the excess soil, and keep them fresh and moist until you replant them simply by covering them up with a sheet of moist newspaper to keep them out of the sun.

STEP 2   Next, rake over the bare patch so that is no longer compacted, and is level and free of weeds.

STEP 3   Replant the runners.

STEP 4   Cover them over with some washed river sand to weigh them down and help keep them moist till they root. Hose the cuttings gently and regularly until they take, then mow along with the rest of your lawn. Soon the patch will be completely covered over.

STEP 4

TOP-DRESSING

There was a time when each spring every homeowner would top-dress their lawn. Thinking these days is that this practice is rarely necessary, and that you only need to top-dress your lawn when it is no longer level. Where this is the case, dips and hollows should be evened out with a top-dressing of coarse washed river sand, cordoned off from pets and foot-traffic and the grass allowed to grow through, then mowed in the usual way.

STEP 1

STEP 2

STEP 3

STEP 1   Empty a bag of washed river sand onto the lowest part of your lawn.

STEP 2   Spread the sand out so that it forms a level 'skin' over the sunken spots. You can either use a wooden float (which is like a broom without bristles) on a handle, or a leaf rake. Try not to cover the grass more than 5 cm (2 in) deep, as you don't want the grass to be 'dead and buried'.

STEP 3   Wait patiently for the runners to grow in from the sides and the grass to come up through the sand. Regular water and mowing on a high setting will work wonders.

KEEPING YOUR GRASS HEALTHY

A lush green lawn underfoot not only looks and feels great, it also sets off your house and garden. Keeping weeds out of your grass used to mean hours of backbreaking hand-weeding, but modern treatments have made bowling green effects attainable for the weekend gardener.

Lawn weeds can be broken into two main categories: annuals, which are spread by windborne seed, like dandelion, plantain and clover; and perennial weeds like oxalis and onion grass, which spread not only by seed but also from persistent bulbils. Control annual weeds by keeping them mown regularly and stopping them from seeding. Stubborn perennial weeds such as onion grass will need spot spraying (see pages 106–7), that is, applying herbicide directly onto their foliage. For grass with bad infestations of broad-leaf weeds such as dandelion and cudweed, consider using sulphate of ammonia and 'lawn sand' to help cure the problem — see pages 104–5.

You can help minimize the spread of weeds into your lawn with these simple measures:

- Raise the height of the mower. Mowing close to ground level increases the risk of weed invasion.
- Mow frequently. This is less stressful for your lawn. Less stress means fewer weeds.
- Aerate your lawn with a garden fork, aerating shoes or a tined garden roller, depending on the size of the lawn. Areas that get heavy use, such as gateways and the track to the clothes line, should be forked over or cored each year.
- Only top-dress when necessary. Imported soil can introduce weeds. Top-dressing is best done only if your lawn is uneven.
- Clean up. If you hire people to mow your lawn, ask them to wash down their mowers before they cut your grass. After all your hard work you don't want to import weeds from other gardens.

MOW FREQUENTLY

AERATE WITH A GARDEN FORK

FEEDING AND LIMING YOUR LAWN

STEP 1

STEP 2

STEP 3

Having taken care of the above points, the next step is to feed your lawn. Hungry grass is slow to repair damage caused by pets, insect attack and active children. Liquid fertilizer will provide an instant pick-me-up, and slow-release fertilizers will provide a safe and sustained supply of nutrients over the rest of the year.

Over time, fertilizing can create an acid soil that prevents many nutrients being fully available to the grass. An annual application of lime will rectify this and sweeten the soil. A simple pH test will show you whether liming is necessary. Always wear gloves, as lime (calcium carbonate) can burn the skin. As with any chemical, only apply in calm weather. Hot windy days can result in burnt grass, health hazards and chemicals leaching into the environment.

STEP 1   Use a pH test kit to check the acidity of the soil, or look for signs of acidity in your garden, such as blue hydrangeas.

STEP 2   If the result shows that the soil is very acid, water the lawn thoroughly first, then apply lime at the rate specified on the bag – about 100 g per square metre (3½ oz per 10¾ ft).

STEP 3   After applying the lime, water the lawn again to prevent burning.

WEED LIQUID FERTILIZER

Weeds have their uses. The weeds you have pulled out can be recycled as a liquid fertilizer to replace nitrogen in the garden. (You can include weeds that have been sprayed with glyphosate as this breaks down quickly in the environment, but don't use weeds that have been sprayed with anything else.) In warm weather it will take only a few weeks for the weeds to break down, in winter rather longer.
STEP 1: Almost fill a plastic garbage bin with weeds. Cover the weeds with water and replace the lid, leaving it a little loose to allow fermentation gases to escape in hot weather. Leave undisturbed in a spot where any smells from the decomposing weeds will not disturb you, until the vegetable matter has disintegrated.
STEP 2: Dilute the resulting thick brown goo 10:1 with water and pour onto the garden using a watering can.

WEEDING

Weeding is the bane of our garden lives. It can seem like an insurmountable task to get on top of weeds, but several simple techniques can make the job at hand easier. The soft fleshy leaves of many annual weeds can be burnt off easily. In paved areas, using boiling water from the kettle is an environmentally sensitive and effective method. Chemically burning off weeds in lawn is also possible using a good dollop of sulphate of ammonia. Another method, practical and useful for large open areas infested with weeds, is to place a black plastic sheet over the offending spot, peg it into place and let the heat of the sun do the job. This is called solar sterilization.

Weedicides are another option. These are particularly effective on persistent weeds which grow from bulbs, including onion weed, nut grass and oxalis. Weedicides such as glyphosate will kill on contact, so be careful to spray only what you intend to kill. Using a brush applicator, a pair of tongs with a sponge, or a weeding wand in densely planted areas will avoid the problem of spray drift damaging 'good' plants. Placing a container over the plants you want to protect will also help. With woody weeds (think privet (*Ligustrum*), Paddy's lucerne (*Sida rhombifolia*) and blackberry), it is often more effective to cut the stem and paint on a mixture of oil (to aid absorption) and poison.

Prune off the flowering and fruiting stems of serious invaders such as privet and pampas grass (*Cortaderia selloana*), even if you can't remove them completely. The most enjoyable method of weed control is to plant more of the plants you want and thus decrease the available space in which weeds can take hold. Aside from these methods, there is always the tried and true — hand-weeding persistently. An oldie but a goodie! Winter grass should be weeded out by hand before it takes over, and many annual weeds can be removed quickly and without fuss by hand.

SIMPLE TECHNIQUES FOR KILLING WEEDS

HAND WEEDING

Many annual weeds, like chickweed (*Stellaria media*), dandelion, purslane and flickweed (*Cardamine hirsuta*), are removed quickly and without fuss by hand. These weeds tend to have non-persistent roots, which don't leave behind propagation material when pulled out. Their main method of spread is by seed, so they tend to be very effective at flowering and dispersing their seeds. If you can remove the flowers, seeds, roots and all by hand, you'll have cheated them out of their next life cycle. This is great when you are dealing with small areas. A liquid fertilizer can be made from weeds pulled this way.

HANdy HINT.

Oxalis comes away easily by hand. Unfortunately it also comes away easily from its bulblets, which you must dig up at the same time to prevent regrowth.

BOILING WATER ON WEEDS

Some very fleshy, soft-leafed weeds can be burnt to death either with chemicals (such as sulphate of ammonia on clover) or even boiling water — think milkweed. You can use boiling water on chickweed too — unless you have visiting or aviary birds, in which case pull the chickweed by hand and give it to them — the birds will love you for it.

BLACK PLASTIC

A very simple and practical method for dealing with larger areas infested with weeds and unwanted grasses, which you may want to turn into a garden bed or a lawn, is to lay a large sheet of black plastic over the offenders, the edges pegged or in some other way held firmly down, and let the hot sun of summer do the trick. Leave in place for a few weeks, and remove. Any weed seeds that have lain dormant may germinate at this stage, so replace the plastic after three or four weeks and repeat the process. This is called solar sterilization.

GARdeNeR'S TiP. Weeds are opportunists, and will take over any bare soil quickly. Don't waste any time in getting new beds planted up, and make sure you mulch thoroughly (see pages 66–7) so you don't have to keep on weeding ad infinitum.

SULPHATE OF AMMONIA

Sulphate of ammonia is quite a strong chemical fertilizer which, applied straight onto broad-leafed weeds, can burn them badly enough to kill them. Whatever product you have left can be mixed with sand and thrown onto the lawn as a fast-acting fertilizer. This is only recommended for occasional use, however, as it can make the soil too acid with repeated applications.

YOU will need.

Gloves

Sulphate of ammonia

Washed river sand

Bucket

Hose

STEP 1

STEP 2

STEP 3

STEP 4

STEP 5

STEP 6

STEP 1   Wearing gloves, apply a handful of sulphate of ammonia directly onto problem spots.

STEP 2   To the remaining sulphate of ammonia, add an equal portion of sharp river sand.

STEP 3   In a bucket, mix well to make 'lawn sand'.

STEP 4   Broadcast the 'lawn sand' over your entire lawn.

STEP 5   Water lightly, taking care not to completely wash the sulphate of ammonia off the weeds.

STEP 6   Blobs of the sulphate of ammonia should remain on the weeds, like this, after the hose-down. This will quickly burn off broad-leaved weeds.

USING WEEDICIDES

SELECTIVE WEEDICIDES

Selective weedicides, which can be used to kill weeds growing among other plants like lawn grasses, are very effective in beating problems such as bindii (*Soliva pterosperma*), paspalum, clover and nutgrass (*Cyperus esculentus*) which can creep into your back lawn and get a hold, especially if the grass is stressed or patchy. Selective weedicides are complex chemicals, and great care needs to be exercised not only in their application, but also in their purchase. The way they are absorbed into turf varies, so it is crucial to make sure you are applying the right chemical for your particular grass type, and to treat your particular weed, or you could end up killing the whole lot, grass and all! Buffalo grass, blue couch and kikuyu are all particularly sensitive. Also, the ratio of chemical to water is crucial, so make sure you use the right concentration. Use only the exact quantity of concentrate specified on the label, as too much can kill off your grass as well! It is essential to treat weeds at the earliest possible stage, when they are young and actively growing: this is when a weedicide is most effective, and is also important for weeds like bindii, as once they have set seed no amount of spray will remove their pesky, pointy seeds.

READ THE LABEL

HAND PUMP

SPRAYING WITH A HAND PUMP

CLOCKWISE FROM TOP LEFT Always read the label to make sure you are using the right amount of concentrate for the right weed! • Pressurizing a hand pump pack • Spraying unwanted paspalum • Using a hose pack to spray bindii killer directly on the lawn.

HOSE PACK

PAINTING WEEDICIDE   SPOT WEEDING   PATH SPRAYING

NON-SELECTIVE WEEDICIDES

Non-selective or less selective weedicides are useful for spot-spraying problem areas or persistent, perennial weeds with corms and bulbs such as nut grass, onion weed (*Asphodelus fistulosus*) and onion grass (*Melica geyeri*). The most commonly used weedicide is glyphosate, and there are other chemicals more suited to woody weeds. The only problem is that they do kill whatever they touch, so the method of application is critical to avoid mishap.

Weeding wands or homemade versions, such as tongs with sponge tips, or paint-brushes, will ensure you poison only what you want to kill. Dye (think virulent blue or red or yellow food colouring) mixed in with the weedicide will stop you doubling up or missing areas, and spray barriers, such as upturned plastic bottles over small, precious seedlings, are a good way of stopping drift.

TOP LEFT TO RIGHT   Painting weedicide on weeds established in cracks in a terrace • Spot weeding a lawn with a weeding wand • Paving is an easier place to control weeds. Here you can spot spray or use a once-a-year path spray (remembering this latter is only an option if tree roots won't be affected).

GARDENER'S TIP. Make sure you don't give clippings treated with weedicide to poultry or other animals. NEVER feed mown grass to any animal, as it may be contaminated with oil or petrol (gasoline) from the mower.

POISONING TREE STUMPS

When a tree has to be cut down, you are often left with the annoying problem of a stump which refuses to accept the sentence, persisting in sending up suckers. The easiest way to deal with this is to poison the stump immediately after it's been cut, while the cut is still green and will easily absorb the weedicide.

STEP 1

STEP 2

STEP 3

STEP 4

STEP 1   To aid the absorption of the weedicide, first pepper the stump with a series of small drill holes.

STEP 2   Brush away the wood shavings to reveal a clean surface, then pour some weedicide carefully over the stump and work it into the holes with a brush.

STEP 3   Next, cover the whole cut with oil (whatever type you have to hand). Mix this with the weedicide, using the same brush, and spread it evenly over the surface.

STEP 4   Occasionally a truly stubborn stump will send up suckers a few weeks later. Brush them with weedicide – you will eventually win.

PEST AND DISEASE CONTROL

Pests and diseases can be controlled to what is known as 'an acceptable tolerance' with organic or low toxic methods. This is by far the best form of management when it comes to home gardening — because your garden should be safe for everyone to enjoy, birds and bees included.

You may find from time to time that your natural garden helpers — insect-eating birds and some insects themselves — aren't up to the task of beating a severe infestation, and you will need to use a pesticide. Before you reach for the chemical ones, however, try the friendlier methods suggested in this section.

HOME REMEDIES

Overcoming problems and outwitting pests has been a continual game of cat and mouse for gardeners, ever since we first started to practise horticulture. Insect plagues of biblical proportions can still dog our attempts at gardening, but now, hopefully, our knowledge of their life cycles and weaknesses means we can outsmart them or at least keep them at tolerable levels.

HANDY HINT.

Praying mantises, green and elegant, are closely related to grasshoppers, stick insects and cockroaches, but are really useful to have around as they feed on other bugs. They quietly stalk their prey and then pounce, using their front legs to hold their dinner. Other beneficial insects in the garden include bees, ladybird beetles (both adults and larvae), hoverflies and spiders.

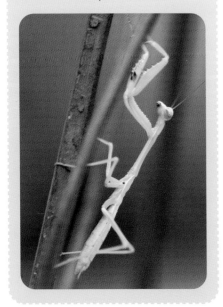

CITRUS BEETLE

CITRUS BEETLES

If your great crop of oranges or lemons has brown, dry pithy sections inside, and fails to live up to expectations, your tree may be under attack from citrus beetles.

Vacuuming might sound strange (and it certainly will look odd), but can be the simplest method of removing citrus beetles (both the spined citrus beetle and the bronze-orange bug) safely. These bugs have a nasty habit of spraying out foul-smelling and toxic liquids if approached, so sometimes wearing gloves and eye protection, and approaching with care, are the best modes of attack — and the long arm of your vacuum cleaner will ensure you are able to keep at a safe distance until they are sucked away.

ANTS

Ants are generally helpful allies in the garden, but sometimes their numbers can reach plague proportions and they become a garden problem. Sap-sucking insects, such as aphids and scale, love ants, because the ants protect them from predators so that they can harvest the sticky honeydew which these insects excrete. Beat the ants at their own game by laying sticky traps of your own. Mix jam (or honey, icing sugar or anything sweet) and borax together and leave out in a shallow bowl protected by a firmly fixed chicken wire or gauze screen that small children, dogs and birds cannot remove. The ants will come and feast on the sweets take some home to their nests, and it's game over!

WHITE FLIES

For some reason white flies, the flying insects that destroy bean and tomato crops, are madly in love with the colour yellow. Sticky yellow paper traps, available from garden centres, can be hung in plants prone to attack, and are sure to get them unstuck!

BIRDS

If birds are causing a nuisance in your fruit trees, tomato plants or berry bushes, try hanging plastic snakes and shining objects (aluminium foil, old CDs) in your trees and trellises. These scare the birds away and can also work well with swimming pools that have ducks migrating into them and causing a mess — a common problem on rural and semi-rural properties. Other deterrents include outline shapes of cats, owls and other predatory birds; sometimes these are also holographic.

SNAILS AND SLUGS

Snails and slugs can be quite a problem, particularly in cool wet weather — being quite voracious where new shoots and seedlings are emerging — not to mention decimating your precious basil plants! You can protect new growth with snail pellets, which must be hidden under heavy pots or inside a piece of terracotta pipe if you have inquisitive children or dogs — or even satin bower birds (the males love anything blue). Snails and slugs love protected spots like this. But you can also try a couple of non-chemical solutions. Snails, at least, will 'drown their sorrows' in a small quantity of beer placed in a saucer on the ground or in a small jar pushed into the soil. Otherwise, collect the snails and slugs by hand (you might prefer to wear disposable gloves while you do this!) and drop them into a bucket of water.

VACUUMING CRITTERS FROM CITRUS IS A SAFE FORM OF PEST CONTROL

CHILLI SOAP SPRAY

YOU WILL NEED: *About 8 red chillies; Bar of soap (or ½ cup pure soap flakes); Grater; Sharp knife; Chopping board; Spray bottle; Water*
Use this environmentally friendly insecticide on a still day so you don't get any in your eyes. Don't be tempted to take a shortcut and use liquid detergent because it will break down the natural waxy coating of a plant's leaves and cause severe damage. Grate the soap and put it (or the soap flakes) in a spray bottle. Half fill with water. Finely chop the chillies, add to the bottle and screw the lid on firmly. Shake vigorously, then use your home-made insecticide on any insect-infested plant.

BIO-INSECTICIDE FOR CATERPILLARS

A bio-insecticide called Dipel (based on the bacterium *Bacillus thuringiensis* var. *kurstaki*) works on certain types of caterpillars. (You will have to check the packaging instructions to confirm whether it works on the caterpillars infesting your plants.) This is a safe and effective method for minimizing damage from these chewing grubs. It's really simple to add a sachet of the powdered bacteria to water, mix thoroughly and spray over any susceptible shrubs or flowers, or use at the first sign of damage.

Another option is chosing a spray product that contails spinosad — which reacts on an insect's nervous system. It affects caterpillars, thrips and some members of the *Diptera* (flies). At this stage it is only registered for caterpillars on fruits and vegies. It has a commercial registration as a fruit fly lure. It is a penetrant, which means that it gets inside the fruit and foliage and doesn't wash off. It is used in many integrated pest management programmes and won't harm beneficial insects like praying mantis.

STEP 1

STEP 2

STEP 3

STEP 1   Add powdered bacteria to some water.

STEP 2   Mix thoroughly and make up to the required quantity.

STEP 3   Spray affected plant thoroughly, making sure to spray the under surfaces of the leaves as well.

FUNGICIDES

Sometimes, especially in the case of fungal infections, such as black spot on roses, petal wilt on azaleas or rust on canna lilies, natural remedies will have little effect and you will have to resort to chemicals. Society garlic (*Tulbaghia violacea*), shown here, is almost always free of pests (due to its garlic scent) but sometimes rots in wet weather, needing a fungicide treatment.

STEP 1

STEP 2

STEP 3

STEP 4

SAFETY PRECAUTIONS

Using chemicals is a task that requires care and exacting applications. Too much or too little may result in the product not working properly or, worse still, cause the user sickness or injury, or pets and wildlife grief and harm – not to mention the risk of burning the plant with too strong an application. Always wear gloves and goggles, and spray only on a still day. Finally, always spray at the distance from the foliage directed on the pack, making sure you get thoroughly under the leaves. Always wash your hands and any other skin that might have been exposed to the spray thoroughly after using any chemical.

Read the label carefully, paying careful attention to the withholding periods (time after spraying when you can eat that plant), warnings about pets, fish or swarming insects, and protective clothing needed.

STEP 1   Use the measure provided, or use a teaspoon and level it to make sure you have a perfect amount every time.

STEP 2   First fill the container you are using to spray (unless the instructions tell you not to) with half the final quantity of water, and add the concentrate to that. This way, if you spill or splash any, it will be partially diluted, not full-strength.

STEP 3   Add the concentrate. Narrow-necked spray bottles are easily filled with a folded piece of paper directing the powder neatly into small openings. Add a final top-up of water and shake well once the top is securely on.

STEP 4   Spray at the distance indicated on the pack, making sure you get thoroughly under the leaves.

SCALE INSECTS AND OIL SPRAY

Bad scale infestations will need to be treated with a combination of white oil and a poison (normally malathion) in order to kill all stages of their life cycle. This can be bought premixed (as we are using here), or you can mix your own. Because a contact poison is being used, wear gloves and spray in still weather. Add the white oil/malathion concentrate to half the specified quantity of water, in case any spills occur, and then top up to the required amount. Shake well.

STEP 1   Measure out the malathion/oil mix in the measure provided with the insecticide, or in a plastic medicine cup kept ONLY for this purpose.

STEP 2   Pour the concentrate into a measuring jug kept ONLY for use with garden poisons, pre-filled with half the total amount of water required, then add the remaining quantity of water. Pour the mixture carefully into the spray container and shake well once the top is securely on.

STEP 3   Spray at the distance from the foliage directed by the instructions, making sure you get thoroughly under the leaves.

STEP 1   STEP 2   STEP 3

A spare 5 minutes.

TABLETS FOR TREES

Trees are often the forgotten plants of our gardens when it comes to fertilizing. An easy once-a-season pick-me-up is an application of pelletized manure tablets. They are simply buried 3–5 cm (1¼–2 in) deep around the drip line, the line to which the tree's canopy extends and where rain drips off, as this is the area where most feeder roots accumulate. They will help improve soil structure, are 100 per cent natural, promote earthworms and are suitable for all trees and shrubs.

BORERS

'Borer' is a generic term for any grub that eats away at trees. Borers can be extremely damaging, even causing ringbarking (the tree equivalent of starving to death) if they manage to eat their way completely around the trunk of a plant. The problem is that borers feed underneath the bark, so often it's hard to spot them until it's too late. For this reason, it's prudent to check over your trees annually – winter is an ideal time as quite a number of plants are bare and more easily examined.

The key indicators of borer are dead wood, die-back and frass (this is the excrement left by boring pests, and looks like chewed-up sawdust and spiders' webs mixed together).

STEP 1

STEP 2

STEP 3

S T E P   1   Scrap away the frass, which will crumble off easily. Closer examination might reveal a small hole, or perhaps several.

S T E P   2   Poke the small-ended hook down the holes.

S T E P   3   If you keep at it, you'll eventually hook up a borer. Eliminate it! Repeat with every hole you find, then remove all traces of frass to leave only clean healthy wood.

YOU WILL NEed.

A scraping tool

A small-ended hook made from a strong wire like piano wire, or a paper clip opened out

GARdeNeR'S TiP. In most cases borers attack trees only when they are stressed. Normally they are smothered by the vigorous flow of sap. Keeping your trees well watered in periods of drought, removing debris and grass from around their bases, pruning branches that rub against each other, and watching that the ground doesn't become overly compacted from heavy foot traffic or parked cars, will all reduce the likelihood of borers making inroads.

GARDEN ORGANIZATION

Like any craft, gardening needs a certain amount of organization to manage all the bits and pieces associated with it — from tools to seeds, to potting-up clutter or watering and feeding gear, there is always plenty of 'stuff' kicking around. Finding a way of organizing everything and a place for it all will help you enjoy your hour in the garden all the more.

GARDENING TOOLS

Gardening is so much more enjoyable if the tools you need are close at hand, and the mess you've created during your hour's work can easily be cleared away. Not everyone has the room for a garden shed these days, but adapting household items and transforming them into garden gems is a simple way of cleaning up your act.

The humble washing basket and trolley make an excellent carry-all, for example. Use the basket itself for bulkier items like loppers, long-handled secateurs, bottles of fertilizer, atomizers and watering cans. Attach a tote bag over the trolley handle and you have a place for personal items like gloves, a kneeling cushion, sunblock and a hat – even a notebook for ideas or a magazine for inspiration. Clothes pegs are great for holding closed half-full seed packets or sample sachets. A garden journal kept in the tote bag is a useful tool for recording successes and failures.

If floor space is at a premium – perhaps you only have a balcony – then why not use the vertical storage space available to you. A shoe organizer makes a great, easily hung carry-all for hand tools, seeds, packets of fertilizer, gloves and so on. Get one that is either transparent or semi-transparent so you can see at a glance what you have and where it is.

YOU WILL NEED.

THE ESSENTIAL GARDENING KIT

Secateurs (garden shears)

Loppers

Gloves

Sunblock

Hat

Basket or other storage of some sort
(like a shopping cart)

Watering can

Atomizer

Measuring jug

Permanent pen or soft pencil

Tags

Trowel

Spade

Weeder

Fork

A spare 5 minutes.

LABELLING

Seeds, bulbs, named varieties and special cultivars all deserve a decent label to keep them identified from one season to the next. If you are using plastic tags, make sure you use a permanent waterproof pen or marker; if you are using metal tags, imprint the name with an empty ballpoint pen; use a 3B or carpenter's pencil on wooden tags.

A WASHING BASKET IS A GREAT CARRY-ALL

BRIGHT COLOURS AND PATTERNS MAKE SPOTTING YOUR GEAR EASIER

CLOTHES PEGS MAKE USEFUL CLIPS

GARDENER'S TIP.

A specially designed bag or tool wrap will not only keep your tools handy, but will also help keep them in good condition – you are far more likely to wipe them before putting them away if they have their own designated space.

GENERAL MAINTENANCE

Much as we all hate mundane work, there are some fairly tedious tasks around the house and in the garden that need repeating on a regular basis. Pulling out weeds that spring up from seeds blown in from elsewhere (they can't come from flowering weeds in your garden, because you've got rid of such unwanted residents), levelling out the mounds of mulch that your beloved cat has piled up in performing its 'business', sweeping paths, cleaning windows and flyscreens (looked at from the outside, they form part of the garden!), scraping moss from damp corners, clearing windblown leaves from protected nooks — all fall into this category. Leaves, moss scrapings and cobwebs can go direct to the compost bin (but there's not much you can do about the cat!).

A good way of removing moss or algal build-ups on paths is to clean them up with a bucket of water and a hard broom. Follow this with a light washdown with diluted chlorine or bleach to help keep them free of growth for longer. You can use this technique on the walls of the house too.

HANdY HiNT.

The leafblower has done wonders for the hard surface once-over. Leafblowers are particularly useful for gravelled or pebbled areas which are difficult to sweep or rake.

HOSES AND TAP FITTINGS

I've wasted too many moments of my life untangling hoses, mending hoses that kinked and split, putting fittings back on when they have blown off the hose, and becoming irritated at having water dribble down my arm when watering. I resolved eventually to purchase the best brass fittings and the best quality hoses, which are less easily kinked, to sort the whole mess out once and for all. The result is a much more pleasurable experience every time I need to water.

STEP 1

STEP 2

STEP 3

STEP 4

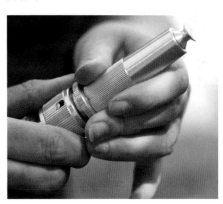

STEP 5

STEP 1   Select the correct gauge brass tap adapter. You can buy various sizes depending on the dimensions of your plumbing, so make sure you measure up before making the trip to the hardware store.

STEP 2   Screw the tap adapter onto the tap.

STEP 3   Thread the first part of the brass hose connector onto the hosepipe, then press the other part of the fitting firmly down into the hose. If you have difficulty getting this bit on, soak the end of the hose in a cup of boiling water to make it softer and more flexible. Screw the two pieces together until tight.

STEP 4   Repeat step 3 on the other end of the hose.

STEP 5   Attach a brass adjustable nozzle so you can turn the water off and on and vary the flow easily.

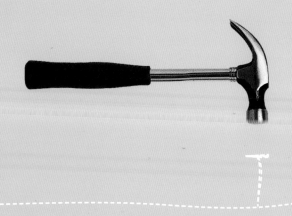

MINI MAKEOVERS

INSPIRING WAYS TO TRANSFORM
A SPOT IN THE GARDEN

COVERED SPACES: MAKING THE MOST OF VERANDAHS AND BALCONIES

Quite often verandahs and balconies that lack privacy become what you might call 'dead zones' — minimalist, bare and sterile. This section is all about making the most out of verandahs and balconies.

With space at a premium in most households, fully utilizing such areas by transforming them into useable 'outdoor rooms' makes sense. With a little thought, the selection and placement of appropriate plants and furnishings will turn dead spaces into welcoming areas where you will enjoy sitting in the evening with a book in one hand and a glass of wine in the other, or spending time with family and friends over a relaxing meal. Adding a glass-walled extension on one side of the house can be another way of creating space, with groupings of plants helping make a seamless transition from the built environment to the garden.

PATIO

Does the entrance to your home let the place down? In this renovated bungalow the front door lacked charm and the semi-enclosed verandah was bleak, to say the least! Two garden seats rescued from the back of the house, some soft furnishings, a number of well-placed plants and an easily-operated bamboo blind in the main 'window' have transformed this lacklustre access-way into a welcoming retreat.

The key issue here was privacy, or rather, the lack thereof. A new building next door faced straight onto the verandah – some sort of screening was essential. Stunning star jasmines (*Trachelosperum jasminoides*), planted in tall pots to give instant height, will be trained with wire to frame the front 'window' as they grow. A few potted plants on the floor, such as a peace lily (*Spathiphyllum*) and a water feature add a serene feel. Elegant hanging pots filled with strings of pearls (*Senecio rowleyanus*) in the front 'window' provide privacy there, pots of tall, spiky chincherinchee (*Ornithogalum thyrsoides*) perform the same function in the side 'window'. To finish, a simple hanging flyscreen for the bedroom door keeps both insects and prying eyes out.

The plain grey concrete floor has been transformed with a coat of dark red paving paint, which adds life to the simple monochromatic colour scheme

PEACE LILY (*SPATHIPHYLLUM*)

STRING OF PEARLS IN DIMPLED CERAMIC POTS

THE VERTICAL LINES OF CHINCHERINCHEE

STAR JASMINE TRAINED UP TALL STAKES FLANKS THE SIDE WINDOW

This left room for the two large seats under the 'windows', and for a redundant side table saved from the tip to live on again. Styling was purposely kept low key, with a slightly masculine feel. Striped cushions in monochromatic greys, khakis and creams were added to give an understated feel and allow details such as the pebble mulches to feature. Texture is the key here, with dimpled pots, crackle glazes and coir door mats highlighted. Even the plants are chosen for their unusual textures, with the round, succulent leaves of the strings of pearls (*Senecio rowleyanus*) contrasting with crinkly, strappy ferns and glossy leaves.

The final touches to this private sanctuary include a restful water bowl with a flowering water lily, and a scattering of scented candles. This position is unique in that this Southern hemisphere home faces south-west, and so gets a shaft of quite strong sunlight through the main opening every afternoon for quite a few hours (the opposite is true in the Northern hemisphere where a north-west aspect would receive this afternoon sun). The rest of the space is protected by the surrounding wall. Lower levels of sunlight would require you to use a different flowering plant, such as arum lily or water poppy.

Timeline Once all the materials and plants had been decided on and brought together, this makeover took only four hours to complete. In the first hour we cleared out what was on the verandah, cleaned it and arranged bench seats and side table and put in place the large, empty pots, including the water bowl – this was then half-filled with water.

It took another hour to put up the bamboo blind and hang the string screen, screw in the hooks for the hanging pots and bring in the bagged potting mix and all the plants.

In the third hour we potted the up star jasmine, golden cane palms, ferns, strings of pearls and flowering bulbs, and placed the aquatics in the half-filled water bowl. The fourth hour saw us sweeping up spillage, top-dressing pots and vases with pebbles, arranging the cushions, filling up the water bowl and watering everything else to settle the plants into their new homes.

HANGING BASKETS

Hanging baskets offer a nice divide between the outside world and the patio space. String of pearls (*Senecio rowleyanus*) with their fragrant cinnamon-like smell add a sense of tranquility to the scene.

STEP 1

STEP 2

STEP 1   Before drilling, mark the hole with a pencil.

STEP 3   Hang the basket.

STEP 2   Using strong self tapping cup hooks, wind them into the hole in a stable piece of hardwood.

A *spare* 5 *minutes*.

WATER BOWL

This water bowl is glazed, so it doesn't need waterproofing. Any large attractive container will do the trick, however, as long as it is waterproofed using a liquid hydrocarbon compound. Once the sealant has fully dried, fill with your choice of aquatic plants, and add a few goldfish to keep mosquito larvae under control.

This bowl contains a grouping of water lilies, *Arum* 'Green Goddess' and striped club rush (*Schoenoplectus lacustris* 'Zebrinus'). A detailed description of how to make a water feature like this appears on page 175.

FLOWERING BULBS

Bulbs are great in pots as they can be displayed in a prominent position when flowering, and tucked away in a quiet corner when they're yet to bud. The beautiful bulbs used here, chincherinchee or star of Bethlehem (*Ornithogalum* sp.), have starry white blooms borne on long stems, and make a pretty feature.

STEP 1

STEP 2

A SPARE 5 MINUTES.

Top-dressing using gravel doesn't have to be kept just for pots. Putting gravel around the candles in hurricane vases is a quick and easy finishing touch which adds a stylish flourish. Nowadays there are many pebbles and decorative gravels to choose from, like the serene green, grey and white used here; shades of pink, yellow, black and terracotta are also available.

STEP 1 Transferring these plants out of uninteresting basic plastic into glossy black-glazed decorative pots really adds to their appeal. Firm down carefully.

STEP 2 Water thoroughly when finished to minimize transplant shock.

FLY SCREEN

A decorative knotted-string screen gives some insect protection and privacy to the front bedroom, which opens onto the verandah, as well as adding to the general style of the makeover.

All it takes is 5 minutes, a pencil and some self-tapping cup hooks.

STEP 1

STEP 2

STEP 3

STEP 1   Mark the position where the cup hooks are to go with a pencil.

STEP 2   Carefully screw the cup hooks in place.

STEP 3   Hang the screen.

VERANDAH

A frequent problem with apartment and balcony living is a lack of privacy. Potted plants can help, but often they are simply not tall enough to reach head height, where you most need screening. This is where hanging baskets — not just one, but several — can be really effective. You can hang them at exactly the right height and spacing to block out unpleasant views or create an intimate nook. Work out the number you need, and buy attractive baskets (we've used woven cane ones here), and strong cup hooks with swivel attachments, which allow you to rotate the plants without taking them down, so that the sun can reach them evenly. Mark their positions and fix them in place as described on page 131 in the patio makeover.

The downside of baskets has always been that they dry out so quickly. The trick is to line baskets with strong plastic, and to choose really hardy trailing plants such as sunjewels (*Portulaca*), verbena, dwarf bougainvilleas and prostrate geraniums (*Pelargoniums*). These plants don't object to drying out slightly between drinks, but you can double the effectiveness of the water you do give them by dosing them up with water-storing crystals when you pot them, or by buying potting mix (compost) with water crystals and slow-release fertilizer already added. Get a decent watering-arm attachment for your hose, or a watering can with a hanging basket rose attachment, and you'll be rewarded with masses of blooms from spring to autumn ... much better than the neighbours' prying eyes.

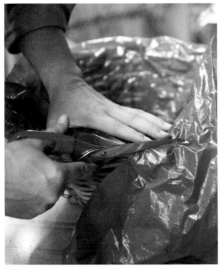

STEP 1

STEP 2

STEP 3

STEP 4

STEP 5

HANdy HiNt.

The more you prune off dead flowers (or bracts, in the case of bougainvilleas), the more the blooms will keep coming. Encouraging horizontal or trailing growth also produces more flowers, as these tend to have more buds than vertical water shoots.

S T E P 1 Line the baskets with plastic (we've opened out a large rubbish bag and cut pieces to fit). This will not only save the baskets, but also stop evaporation around the root zone. Punch a few holes in the base for drainage.

S T E P 2 Hydrate some water crystals and add them to the potting mix in each basket.

S T E P 3 Plant up the baskets with your chosen trailing plants. Here I have used dwarf bougainvillea, a thornless cultivar called 'Bambino Miski'.

S T E P 4 Prune off any leaders that threaten to shoot up vertically — you want to encourage a trailing effect.

S T E P 5 Water in and mulch with decorative pebbles or coloured sand before hanging the basket.

CONSERVATORY

A conservatory, glasshouse or sunroom like this one gives gardeners greater scope to enjoy plants in all weather and climes. This glass-walled conservatory extension has not only added another room to this house, but has also given the owner a place to over-winter frost-sensitive plants, raise seedlings for a jump start on spring sowing and show off some precious gems.

The plain concrete floor was tiled with durable terracotta tiles, sealed and waxed to cope with any water and dirt from the plants and make clean-up easy. Next, an old wicker setting was given a new lease of life with some repainting and simple repair work. A stack of old terracotta pots, mismatched but with great character, were potted with some treasures and the new outdoor—indoor space was complete.

Timeline Although not actually part of the makeover as described here, the first step was to lay the floor tiles on a concrete base. This took half a day, then another half day to grout and seal. Three coats of wax were then applied the following day, a few hours apart.

In the first hour of the actual makeover, the wicker furniture was prepared for painting and the first spray coat applied. In the second hour all the plants were potted up, mulched and watered in. The third hour was taken up in touching up the tricky bits on the furniture and applying a second spray coat, then, when this was touch dry, placing the furniture in position and arranging the plants for the best effect.

WICKER FURNITURE

As with any natural material, from time to time you'll need to give it some maintenance. This garden furniture, made out of wicker, has been let go – but not so far that it can't be restored and brought back into use. It's cheap to pick up cast-offs like this – you can even get them in council clean-ups or rubbish tips — and bring them back to life.

STEP 1

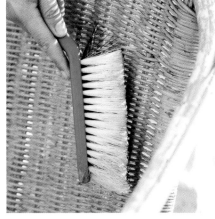

STEP 2

STEP 3

STEP 4

STEP 5

HANDY HINT.

Use glue to stick down any loose ends of wicker before you start to paint the setting.

STEP 1   Scrape off any loose paint from the framework using a wire brush – the sort you use for cleaning a barbecue. Work along the length of the frames to lessen any wear or tear.

STEP 2   Brush down the woven parts, front and back, with a soft dustbrush to remove any loose particles.

STEP 3   Using an aerosol can of gloss white enamel, give the whole setting a once-over. Work from side to side, and then up and down, over the wicker to ensure complete coverage. Old wicker is very 'thirsty', and this first coverage will undoubtedly look somewhat uneven. Don't worry.

STEP 4   Any hard-to-reach spots can be touched up using a brush and matching paint.

STEP 5   Once the paint is dry, apply a second coat.

PLECTRANTHUS 'CREEPING CHARLIE'
VARIEGATED FORM

POT PLANT SELECTION

When choosing plants for a small space it makes sense to limit yourself to a small range of colours. If you don't do this, the space can easily be overwhelmed and turn into a technicolour disaster.

The theme for this conservatory was dictated by the terracotta floor tiles and Western red cedar timber cladding, both of which are in shades of orange. A toned-down orange scheme of pale apricots, white, red and peachy pinks blends beautifully with the hard materials. Don't be afraid of experimenting with leaf colours and textures too. Many indoor and shadehouse plants like begonias, plectranthus and peperomias come in an array of cultivars with fantastic coloured leaves that have an almost stained glass quality about them.

For perfume, a fragrant vireya rhododendron, an unusual white clerodendrum (*Clerodendrum nutans*) and *Hoya carnosa* have been chosen. The latter two are climbers and will be trained up light poles to frame the windows.

VIREYA RHODODENDRON 'KISSES'

CLERODENDRUM NUTANS IS AN
UNUSUAL WHITE FORM OF BUTTERFLY
CREEPER

SUNJEWELS ARE A HARDY SUCCULENT
WITH GREAT SUMMER AND AUTUMN
FLOWERS

GARDENER'S TIP. The pots have all been placed directly on the floor, without saucers underneath them, because the tiled surface is both waterproof and washable, and plants prefer to be in a free-draining situation. If saucers are essential, place a few pebbles or a layer of gravel in them so the pots are lifted up above any reservoir of water.

Don't over-pot your plants. By this I mean don't overwhelm them by using too large a pot. Just go up a size or two from the original pot, allowing at most 5 cm (2 in) extra in depth and all around the circumference of the old pot. Using too large a pot can mean that the potting mix goes 'sour' (anaerobic) waiting for the plant to grow into it.

STEP 1

STEP 2

STEP 3

STEP 1   With old terracotta pots like these, you will often find that the drainage hole is too large and that you need to add either some crocking (broken bits of pot and gravel) or gauze to stop the potting mix from falling straight through the hole. Crocking is sometimes thought of as a means of improving drainage, but in fact it just acts as a false bottom.

STEP 2   Gently tease out any tangled roots, being careful not to damage them. Position the plants carefully in their new homes, and backfill with potting mix.

STEP 3   Mulch with gravel to stop weeds from finding a home and 'dress' your pots nicely.

HOYA CARNOSA AND *ABUTILON*

BALCONY

This small balcony was crying out for a mini makeover. The main access is via a door leading from the kitchen, making it perfect for outdoor eating. The balcony faces the next-door neighbour's garden, which means it needs some privacy, but because it also lets the morning sun in the kitchen windows, anything bulky would darken the room too much.

HANDY HINT.

Lighting doesn't have to be complicated or require an electrician ... in fact, lighting is one of those rare elements that can change the mood of a setting and add its own ambience. Candlelight is not only one of the most primitive forms of lighting, it is also one of the most romantic. Taking a couple of candelabra outside adds a touch of decadence and glamour that is sure to spark some romance.

The rest of the garden is quite formal, with hedges and topiary a feature, so this theme was followed on the balcony, but given an elegant edge suited to dining. Twisted metal candelabra with three-pronged bases were shaped with ivy, and combined with crystal and cast iron candlesticks and a fluted limewashed terracotta pot filled with more ivy to give the marble-topped table a welcoming look. In one corner a small occasional table, also marble topped, is home to a mini hedge of box. A rusted iron pot filled with succulents planted through the lattice takes up another corner.

A graceful variegated ornamental ivy is trained up a metal obelisk for some extra privacy, and hanging baskets filled with Boston fern add just the right amount of screening without blocking out light.

The dining table and slatted chairs were small restoration jobs. The marble table top was badly stained, but some determined work with cleaning products achieved a miraculous result. The chairs were in desperate need of a coat of paint, and had to be cleaned and touched up to make the grade. Every effort was made, however, to retain their heritage colours and old world charm.

Timeline The first step was to prepare the furniture. This was done over a few hours on the two days prior to the rest of the makeover, to allow for drying time. On the day itself, the first hour was spent placing the furniture and repotting the ornamental grape and threading it onto its tripod. The second hour was spent in making up the ivy candelabra and ivy urn. The final hour was taken up in potting up and hanging the fern baskets, potting the decorative latticed urn with succulents, and arranging everything 'just so' on the tables.

RESTORING OLD CHAIRS

STEP 1   STEP 2   STEP 3

STEP 1   Wash and scrub down the old furniture to remove any flaking paint and dirt. Badly worn furniture may need a rub with a wire brush and a once-over with sandpaper.

STEP 2   When thoroughly dry, spray all surfaces with an aerosol primer. You can get products that are suitable for timber as well as metal, which is the easiest option. This colour is red oxide.

STEP 3   Using outdoor grade semi-gloss paint, and a bristle brush, paint the wooden slats. We've chosen mustard yellow to go with the table base, which has remnants of this colour, and also ties in with the paintwork on the house. Allow to dry overnight, then apply a second coat, and a third coat the next day if it's needed. The metalwork was simply left primed, because we found the colour so attractive (other colours are available if you don't like red oxide).

IVY TOPIARY CANDELABRA

STEP 1

STEP 2

STEP 3

HA*ndy* H*i*n*t*.
Keep the new growth of the ivy in check by continuing to cover the candelabra. Once you have enough coverage, just trim off excess growth with scissors.

STEP 4

STEP 5

STEP 1   Plant a fine-leafed form of English ivy (*Hedera helix* 'Smithii', which has five-lobed leaves, is used here) into a suitable pot (we used terracotta). Remember that the finished topiary will be quite top-heavy, so don't underdo the size of the base.

STEP 2   Firmly insert one of the candelabra into the centre of the pot. You can buy these in nurseries, or make one yourself if you're handy with wire and pliers.

STEP 3   Working with one or two of the longest strands, start making your topiary by twisting the ivy round and round the wire stem to the top, then work out along the horizontal to one of the candle bases. If the strands are long enough, work back to cover the last bit of the stem.

STEP 4   Take the next longest pieces and twist them up the stem in the opposite direction, to help lock it all in place. When you reach the top, work out to the candle base on the opposite side.

STEP 5   If there are strands left over, and the top of the stem is still bare, work up the stem again to the very top. Water in well. Now you're ready to add the candles.

HANGING FERN BASKETS

Ferns in containers are notorious for drying out, especially in hanging baskets where they are exposed to the breeze. To help slow down the rate of watering, and to extend the lifespan of your basket, either buy baskets already plastic lined, or line them yourself – see page 135.

The Boston or fishbone fern (*Nephrolepis exaltata*) is one of the hardiest of ferns, suitable for cool to warm climates – so hardy, in fact, that it can become a nuisance in the garden in humid areas. It does, however, have lovely arching fronds which cascade beautifully, making it ideal for baskets. Choosing a decorative basket is important for hanging plants, as they are quite often close to eye-level, so look for something a little special.

STEP 1

STEP 2

STEP 3

STEP 4

STEP 5

HANdy HiNT.

Ferns love frequent watering, and also benefit from regular liquid feeding. If your Boston fern ever dries out badly or begins to look tatty, you can cut it back quite hard, feed and water it — and you'll have a fresh fern again in weeks.

STEP 1   Remove two of the chains from the basket to make your repotting job easier. This ready-lined basket is made from wicker and twine.

STEP 2   Put enough potting mix (compost) in the basket to bring the planted fern up to the right level. Special fern mix, which has extra peat to improve water-holding capacity, is ideal, or you can add some peat to standard mix.

STEP 3   Transfer the fern into the basket and fill around it with more potting mix.

STEP 4   Replace the chains in the appropriate position.

STEP 5   Hang the fern basket in place and water the fern in well (see page 131 for instructions).

ORNAMENTAL GRAPE

This superb ornamental grape (*Ampelopsis glandulosa* var. *brevipedunculata* 'Elegans') is a far more restrained grower than the traditional ornamental grape (*Vitis* sp.), making it perfect for small balconies and pots. It has the added bonus of pretty white variegations on the leaves and exquisite turquoise-blue berries, or 'grapes'. It was transplanted from another section of the garden into this lovely old concrete pot with peeling green paint, which marries perfectly with the foliage. Unless you have really powerful muscles, or a friend who can help with the move, do this job in the pot's final position, because concrete pots are really heavy.

STEP 1

STEP 2

STEP 3

STEP 4

STEP 5

STEP 1   Maintaining the same soil depth, pot up the ornamental grape.

STEP 2   Top up with extra potting mix (compost).

STEP 3   Insert the wire obelisk into the pot, carefully directing all the tendrils into the centre of the frame.

STEP 4   Thread the tendrils back out and around the wire.

STEP 5   Water in well, and move the pot into position.

IVY URN

Using a miniature-leaved ivy adds to the elegant look of the table arrangement. The delicate leaves of the five-lobed English ivy (*Hedera helix* 'Smithii') are shown to advantage against the solidity of the metal urn. The trailing strands can be snipped off if they become too rampant for their situation.

STEP 1

STEP 2

STEP 3

STEP 4

STEP 5

STEP 1   The smaller the pot plant, the more dependent it is on proper care, so make sure you use a quality potting mix.

STEP 2   Gently loosen the rootball. This encourages new root growth in the plant's new home.

STEP 3   Firm down the potting mix with your finger tips to work out any air pockets.

STEP 4   Water in thoroughly.

STEP 5   Mulch with fine gravel, in this case a soft blue shade.

BLOCKOUTS: NOVEL WAYS OF TREATING SCREENS, WALLS AND FENCES – DIVIDE AND CONQUER

Privacy is an important issue in modern society, as more and more people crowd into our cities and houses are built ever closer together. Even within the happiest household, too, people living peacefully cheek by jowl can still feel the need for their own private place at times. Divisions can be more than just boundaries … just as a house has more than four walls, fences, screens and walls can be used internally to break up space in a garden into more useable areas, each with their own clearly defined function. They can also be used as an effective focal point in their own right. Painting them an eye-catching colour, adding an interesting texture or perhaps giving them a sense of folly, as seen in the flower pot fence, are all ways of having fun. Plants can help decorate these divisions, or form the basis of the divisions themselves. The ambience they provide makes even the most solid wall feel less like a jail and more like a sanctuary.

BUDDHA'S HEAD GARDEN

CROTON, A TOUCH OF COLOUR BESIDE
THE DREAMING BUDDHA

The look for this garden began with the owners themselves. The Art Deco-style semi had been modernized by the young couple, with rooms opened up to form an open-plan layout. They had taken the open-plan idea into the garden too, and completed the hard landscaping (construction of a blade wall and wooden banquet seats), but needed some help with the soft landscaping to make the spaces more inviting. The important interior colours were chocolate brown and dove grey with bright red accents, obvious choices for continuation into the garden, especially as the blade wall was already painted red.

The design challenges here are typical of long narrow blocks. Such a space can often look like a shooting gallery, a feeling only accentuated by planting the old 'short back and sides' – the gardening equivalent of long straight hair on a thin narrow face. The trick is to divide up the length into garden rooms, and link them together with glimpses and features so you are drawn to venture to the furthest point.

Integral to the design of this garden was the blade wall, with its fireplace 'window' and firewood-filled 'peep holes', about one-third of the way down. The fireplace is fully functional, with a simple iron grate holding the burning logs, and storage for kindling and its display built into the wall itself. The wall was rendered with tinted render, rather than painted, so that the colour was permanent and heat resistant. Between this wall and the house lay bare earth with weeds and a few clumps of couch grass.

Behind the blade wall was a paved eating area with wooden furniture and two large built-in wooden banquette seats, one of them parallel to the wall, and behind that an area of rather tired lawn with the clothes line and compost bin. The space was thus divided into three distinct 'rooms'. There wasn't much else apart from several established clumps of umbrella grass (*Cyperus alternifolius*).

THE FIRST ROOM, BEFORE AND AFTER

The challenge was to soften these bare bones, achieved through mulching, the use of a variety of colourful, fine-leaved and strappy-leaved plants, and distinctive accessories.

Some months down the track, the owners say the makeover has changed the way they live. They now spend nearly all their home-time outdoors. The other surprising thing is how well it has worn. Despite the dog, the grass and mulch are holding up really well.

Timeline The whole process took less than a day to achieve once we had decided what to do and bought the required plants, pots and accessories. The first hour was clean-up, which entailed a trip to the rubbish tip and a place set aside alongside the cubby house at the bottom of the garden to keep the necessary stuff properly stacked away out of sight. The next hour comprised of weed removal and renovating bare patches in the lawn, the third mulching and the fourth planting. After this, styling the space with feature pots and other accessories took up another hour.

WEEDING AND CLEARING

Having a 'clean slate' doesn't necessarily mean pulling out every living thing and starting with a blank canvas. Often there are plants in a garden that can be utilized, either in their current position or by transplanting them. Removing weeds, however, is a must, as you will never have success with new plantings if they have to compete for water and nutrients with weeds.

Fortunately, the weeds here consisted mainly of residual couch grass, which can be poisoned with a topical application of glyphosate, and *Tradescantia fluminensis*, which comes out easily by hand, but will need to be poisoned if it reshoots. There were also a few annual weeds which, so long as they haven't yet set seed, are reasonably easy to remove.

MULCHING

Once weeds have been dealt with, the only sure way of stopping them reappearing is to mulch the ground, in this case with a thick layer of forest fines (hardwood cut into tiny pieces), which forms a great, hard-wearing base. This is classified as softfall for playground equipment, making it perfect for babies and dogs alike. Make sure the mulch is a good 10 cm (4 in) thick, and reapply it annually to keep it effective. We used it as groundcover in the first room and continued it alongside the eating area in the second room.

Mulch on garden beds can be applied either before or after planting, but will need to be scraped aside from any holes for the planting process. It is light and easy work for anyone – even children can help out!

SHOVELLING MULCH

GARDENER'S TIP. Walls like this one are also useful for hiding utilities, such as this clothes line or a bin and compost.

TRANSPLANTING UMBRELLA GRASS

The umbrella grass was divided up and used as a foil for the stone-look water bell and ball in the first room, and as a backdrop to the Buddha head in the third room. We used the remainder to screen a water tank at the side of the cubby house.

STEP 1

STEP 2

STEP 3

STEP 1   Using a spade to get underneath the roots, lever a section out of the ground.

STEP 2   Carry the division to its new home. Large sections or whole plants may need to be transported in a barrow.

STEP 3   Remove any damaged or dead growth. Umbrella grass is so hardy that you can just pull bits off by hand, but less vigorous plants require more precision, so use secateurs (garden shears).

STEP 4   Place the division in the hole you've dug for it and backfill with some soil from the garden.

STEP 3

OTHER PLANTINGS

The plants used in this makeover were chosen to meet three criteria – the first was foliage colour, the second was ease of care, the third was child friendliness – no poisonous, prickly or allergy-inducing plants here.

In the first room, coleus (*Coleus* x *hybridus*) were used for their great splashes of leaf colour – fabulous pink and rust colours. Two ornamental grasses, purple-leaved fountain grass (*Pennisetum setaceum* 'Rubrum') and zebra grass (*Miscanthus sinensis* 'Strictus') add to the dynamic flowing feeling, and yet still are soft to the touch. In the third room, framing the Buddha head, canna lilies, or Indian shot flower (*Canna* x *hybrida*), provide intense bursts of leaf and flower colour throughout summer and autumn, and the deep red ixora, or flame of the woods (*Ixora coccinea*), adds that wow! factor. *Pittosporum tenuifolium* 'James Stirling' against the fence on the right in the second room, and black bamboo (*Phyllostachys nigra*), contained in pots on the left, screen out the neighbours, and soften the paling fence. Sacred bamboo (*Nandina*) was used on the perimeter of the third room.

UMBRELLA GRASS, CANNAS AND CROTONS AROUND THE BUDDHA'S HEAD

PURPLE-LEAVED FOUNTAIN GRASS

PITTOSPORUM TENUIFOLIUM 'JAMES STIRLING'

GARDENER'S TIP. Put a plastic pot upside down in the base of very tall pots so you use less potting mix.

STEP 1

STEP 2

STEP 3

STEP 4

STEP 5

STEP 6

STEP 1   In the first room, we positioned the plants, still in their pots, to make sure we were happy with the layout before planting them out.

STEP 2   Dig the planting holes one by one and set the soil aside in an unused plastic pot.

STEP 3   Remove the plant (in this case zebra grass) from its pot, loosen the soil around its roots, and position in the hole. Tip the pot of soil back into the hole – much easier than spading it in.

STEP 4   Coleus will add some contrasting colour to the setting and is planted slightly apart.

STEP 5   A small pot of baby's tears (*Helxine* sp.), which will spread and form a living groundcover, is added beside the stone ball. Tidy the mulch and then water in the plants.

STEP 6   Keep going until all the plants are in place.

FEATURE POTS

Many architectural or statement plants are sharp or pointy. Such plants were out of the question in this garden, due to the child-friendly requirement. Instead, bronze-leafed flax (*Phormium tenax* cv) was planted in the tall stone-look pots. Because of the need to keep the garden child friendly, normal bougainvilleas were not appropriate because of their thorns. The bougainvillea in the second room, sold under the name 'Bambino Miski', is a thornless type ideally suited to container growing. For extra blooms, apply sulphate of potash each season and, if growing in the garden, apply manure yearly.

A spare 5 minutes.

SOFT FURNISHINGS

The soft furnishings were chosen to reflect the interior decor of the house, and are stored inside the banquet seats when not in use. An unusual mix of Asian crockery and zany stripes in liquorice all-sorts colours works well and adds a touch of whimsy.

RED WALL: ADDING COLOUR TO YOUR GARDEN

Adding colour to your garden used to be a matter of planting flowers, but now, with some great new products at your disposal, a coat of paint can give your place an extra lift.

Here, a plain bagged brick wall behind a narrow garden bed is given the once-over with a grainy-textured exterior paint. The screening trees used here are an Australian native lilly pilly (*Syzygium leuhmanni*), which has beautiful red berries and pretty deep pink new growth, which will match the red wall superbly. They are underplanted with the pink dwarf kangaroo paw Bush Gem 'Bush Pearl'. In the northern hemisphere garden, photinia can be planted to create the same dramatic splash of red.

HANDY HINT.
Trimming your plants regularly will encourage new growth, which in this case is pretty pink.

STEP 1

STEP 2

STEP 3

STEP 4

STEP 5

STEP 6

STEP 1   Clean the wall thoroughly and remove grime and grit.

STEP 2   Use either a paint roller (which is fastest) or brush (which gets into the gaps best) to apply a coat of acrylic exterior paint. The paint used here is one of the texture-filled Tuscan-look paints which give a grainy, rendered appearance.

STEP 3   After waiting four hours, use a brush to apply a second coat, this time with a criss-cross action.

STEP 4   The wall should be touch dry in another hour or thereabouts, so it's not long before you can think about planting up the garden bed. Add compost to rejuvenate the soil.

STEP 5   Plant out the lilly pillies and water in.

STEP 6   Plant out the kangaroo paws, water in and mulch.

POT FENCE FOR A VEGETABLE GARDEN

Garden fences come in all shapes and sizes, from the simplest picket or wire fence to a grandiose stone or brick wall. The materials used in a fence should reflect the purpose of the area it surrounds, and the nature of the architecture of the building. When it comes to internal fences, or demarcations within a space, however, there is plenty of scope for following through with a fanciful idea and having some fun.

HA*nd*y H*in*T.

Treating hardwood stakes – indeed, any wooden post placed directly into the ground – with a preservative like creosote or sump oil will extend their lifespan.

The home vegetable garden shown here was crying out for some definition from the surrounding yard, but anything too serious would have looked out of place. The solution was to use 1.2 m (4 ft) hardwood tomato stakes – perfectly at home in the vegie patch – as the boundary. These are capped off with small terracotta pots, simply as a folly.

The first requirement is to mark out the line you want the fence to follow. This can be done with a string to give a straight line or, as I did here, marked out by eye to create a slightly haphazard, less formal effect – whichever you prefer.

STEP 1

STEP 2

STEP 3

STEP 1   Using a lump hammer, drive the stakes firmly into position, keeping them as upright as possible.

STEP 2   Continue along the line as needed. The stakes don't have to be the same height.

STEP 3   Top off each stake with a small terracotta pot.

GARDeNeR'S TiP.   If you want to grow tomatoes, beans, peas or sweet peas along the perimeter of the garden, use taller stakes, and if necessary attach some chicken wire to allow them to climb more readily.

BAMBOO CORNER

Bamboo is the perfect plant for screening where narrow beds restrict the width to which a plant can grow, and yet height is required to block out bad views, as was the case here. For a completely minimalist, Zen look, the simplicity of black bamboo (*Phyllostachys nigra*) is hard to beat.

Bamboo requires regular, deep watering, so a manure-enriched compost, which helps hold water in the soil, was used for planting, and plenty of mulch added to stop evaporation.

The Zen picture was completed by repotting an old cycad into a stunning black terrazzo cube.

BAMBOO

The problem with black bamboo is that it is one of the running types, which means it has to be contained either by planting it into raised garden beds (with no way of escape), using a root control barrier or keeping it in pots. Luckily, this bed is built in, and on the other side of the fence there is a 2 m (6½ ft) drop, stopping the roots from travelling.

HANDY HINT.

Black-stemmed bamboo looks particularly good planted in front of a light-coloured wall, which contrasts well and adds impact.

STEP 1

STEP 2

STEP 1   Arrange plants evenly across the space needing to be screened. The bamboo will run, spreading to fill any gaps.

STEP 2   Your instant screen – nothing could be simpler!

CYCAD

This cycad had been sitting around for some time in the garden, but it just wasn't living up to its potential. Its new home, a black terrazzo pot, is tall and heavy, and will be even heavier filled with plant and potting mix, so you can put an upturned plastic container inside to give it a false bottom and make it lighter to move about.

STEP 1

STEP 2

THE OLD CYCAD NOW HAS PRIDE OF PLACE AS A PRIZED SPECIMEN

STEP 3

STEP 4

STEP 1   Cut off the roots protruding through the drainage holes of the plastic pot and remove the cycad.

STEP 2   Put enough potting mix in the pot to bring the cycad to the right finished height and position the plant. Trim off the old fronds, and remove any dried-off or damaged growth to reveal a clean trunk.

STEP 3   Backfill around the cycad, ensuring the roots are covered with potting mix at the same level as before. Building up above this level can cause rotting.

STEP 4   Water well and top-dress with black, glossy pebbles to finish off the look and transform the corner into something tranquil and luscious.

TRANSFORMATIONS: FIXING PROBLEM SPOTS

Often the biggest difference you can make to a garden is quite simple — just pick its worst feature and fix that. It might be where the rubbish bins lurk — screen them with a couple of tall plants — or piles of kids' toys constantly littering a lawn or the patio, where simply creating some form of storage will be the answer. Re-turfing a tatty lawn or mulching a garden bed where groundcover plants have failed can be really cheap ways of changing woe into wow. Even that dead zone of dry and dusty side passage between house and fence need not be a lost cause. If problems are numerous and resources are limited, start with the most visible areas, like the entranceway, the front path and garden beds, then work your way out into the 'living rooms' of your garden.

FRONT GARDEN

The stark, modern façades of many of today's new buildings lend themselves to the reinterpretation of the drought-proof garden, this time with a less bushy, more cutting edge feel. The same plants are often used, but are now planted in more structured ways, sometimes in grid patterns or, as has been done here, in diagonal stripes or bands. This is perfect in gardens which are also viewed from above, as is the case here, and also helps with the geometry and balance of the garden.

The main feature of this garden is two mature grass trees (*Xanthorrhea arborea*). Grass trees have the most marvellous silhouette that makes them perfect as architectural plants, especially when featured against a smooth flat wall of painted concrete. Other drought-tolerant plants that can be used

HANDY HINT.

If a planting hole is greater in depth than 30 cm (12 in), it is important not to add organic matter before you plant, because it can become anaerobic (and dangerous to the plant) as it decomposes without oxygen below the surface. If soil improvement is an issue, use inorganics such as gypsum to break up clay, or plant the specimen in a raised mound to improve drainage.

to similar dramatic effect are Dracaena or Yuccas. The steepness of the site was counterbalanced by using grass trees of different heights, visually evening the slope. A small hedge of a low-growing, bright green-leafed form of coast rosemary (*Westringia longifolia* 'Snowflurry') at the back of the garden forms the rear wall, and will be trimmed on the level as it grows to give a more horizontal feel to the garden.

The rest of the garden is filled with textural plants, the strappy-foliaged blue-leafed flax lily *Dianella caerulea* 'Cassa Blue', and the kangaroo paws Bush Gem 'Gold Nugget' and 'Yellow Gem', both with golden yellow blooms and lime green foliage. These are planted in bands running diagonally across the rectangular garden bed. Groundcovering paper daisies (*Helichrysum apiculatum*) will eventually disguise the drainage grate in one corner, and cascading creeping boobialla (*Myoporum parvifolium*) will spill over the sandstone retaining wall. Many plants from other southern hemisphere or Mediterranean climates are also drought tolerant and provide a similar effect. Think herbs and perennials from the Mediterranean, like lavender, rosemary and thyme, and plants from the Cape in South Africa, like African daisies, gazanias, proteas and leucospermums.

TIMELINE This is a small area, and with all materials assembled it took only two hours to complete the makeover. The first hour saw all the plants, grass trees included, positioned and planted. In the second hour the lines for the lighting were run and the uplights placed for best effect, the drainage pit covered and the whole garden mulched and watered in.

PLANTING OUT LARGE POTTED PLANTS

The most important thing in dealing with a big plant is to dig an oversized hole ... it's much easier, when handling large plants such as these grass trees, to over-dig the hole than to get the plant into position and then realize the hole isn't deep enough! Use a measure to ensure the hole is deeper than the pot the plant is in, then backfill slightly so that the plant ends up at the right height.

STEP 1

STEP 2

STEP 3

S T E P 1   Using all the extra muscle you can muster, have one person hold the trunk and leaves off the ground, even prop it up with something like this recycling box, while another one or two get some purchase on the pot to pull it off the rootball. If necessary, tap the pot with the back of a spade to help loosen it.

S T E P 2   Carefully roll the grass tree into the hole.

S T E P 3   Position the grass tree upright and check from all angles that it is straight before backfilling the hole. Follow the same procedure with the other grass tree.

PLANTING DROUGHT-PROOF PLANTS

Planting out often requires some extra nutrients, soil conditioner or organic matter to be dug in to improve the soil. In this garden, however, the existing soil is very poor and sandy, which is exactly right for the Australian natives used, which love great drainage and low nutrient levels.

STEP 1

STEP 2

STEP 3

STEP 4

STEP 1   Position the plants and make sure you are happy with their layout – it's easier to move them about when they're still in their pots than after they're planted!

STEP 2   Starting with the biggest plants (the coast rosemary) at the back and working down to the smallest at the front (flax lilies and kangaroo paws), begin digging holes and planting.

STEP 3   Make sure that the plants are not buried too deeply as most drought-proof plants are prone to crown rot if their crown is too far below the soil. You should be able to still see the potting mix the plants were originally potted into.

STEP 4   Mulch the garden to a depth of 10 cm (4 in) and water well.

GARDENER'S TIP. Caring for kangaroo paws is no great mystery. They love good drainage and plenty of sunshine, and will flower more if regularly deadheaded. When a flowerstalk finishes producing blooms, cut it off at its base.

DRAINAGE PITS

Builders and renovators these days are required by many local authorities to install huge grated drainage pits to catch run-off. They can look very ugly, but it's a simple matter to cover them up with a piece of fibrous cement, and mulch over the top. Access is easy when necessary, but the pit remains hidden from view the rest of the time.

An extra to this, or an alternative if you prefer, is to plant groundcovers beside the pit, like this yellow creeping paper daisy (*Helichrysum apiculatum*), which will grow over the grid and can be easily lifted if inspection is necessary.

FIBROUS CEMENT CUT TO SIZE AND COVERED WITH MULCH DISGUISES AN UGLY DRAINAGE PIT

YELLOW PAPER DAISY HIDES THE PIT AND ALSO MAKES A PRETTY GROUND COVER

GARDEN LIGHTING

For plants with such fabulous architectural outlines as the grass trees in this makeover, it makes sense to make a feature of their form both day and night. Uplighting was installed by simply running low voltage wires under the mulch once the garden was planted.

They uplight the fabulous grass tree trunks, then silhouette them against the rendered wall.

SIDE PASSAGE

In many gardens the path down the side of the house can turn into 'terrain vague' – a nowhere land with no beauty, a spot to store the bins and not much else. While access will almost always be the main priority, there is no reason you can't turn a bit of wasteland into a feature worth the journey. Small spaces like this are best kept simple in design, so repetition of an element is a useful technique – this will accentuate the length and any feeling of movement. Decking provides an easy thoroughfare, especially if you have to wheel the bins through to the street, and leaving a narrow gap between house and path, or path and fence, gives you the opportunity to plant. Running the boards across the path, as was done here, makes the space appear wider than it actually is.

If you do go with wooden decking, make sure the wood is treated for outdoor use, laid with enough of a slope to drain quickly, and protected from wet ground by a waterproof membrane.

The plants you use will have to be carefully selected for the conditions prevailing in your side passage. Is it a chilly wind tunnel, catching every local breeze and gale? Try cast-iron plant (*Aspidistra elatior*), known to grow anywhere. Is it poorly drained, perhaps a bit soggy? Sedge grass (*Carex*), as seen here, may be the way to go. Is it a hot, dry sun-trap? Try a line-up of hardy succulents, or gazanias, geraniums (*Pelargonium*) and daisies, which love the sun, and in this case think drip irrigation. If the space is so narrow that you can't afford to use any of it for plants, pave or deck the walkway, and consider painting the side fence a cheerful colour, trying your hand at a mural, or attaching some colourful Mexican plaques to add a bit of life.

TIMELINE This makeover was done in an hour.

STEP 1

STEP 2

STEP 3

STEP 1   When planting against a building, make sure that you don't build up soil over the dampcourse (seen here as a black line at the foot of the wall), because this can cause no end of structural problems. Space your selected plants evenly.

STEP 2   Using a quality potting mix (compost), fill in around your chosen plants – in this case, variegated sedge grass (*Carex* sp.).

STEP 3   Brush any spilt potting mix into the garden bed, mulch to a depth of 10 cm (4 in) and water in.

GARDENER'S TIP. Other vertically oriented plants for narrow areas include 'Sacred bamboo' (*Nandina domestica*), espaliered camellias (see page 34) and other climbers.

POOLSIDE

Planting around swimming pools always needs careful consideration. First, there is the effect on the plants of the splash factor from salt water or chlorine to be considered, then the issue of debris dropping into the pool, and the need to avoid thorns which might hook the bare flesh of unwary swimmers.

Like a lot of pools, this one has a paved surround, with not much space left for plants either, and a desperate need for some shade from the hottest of the afternoon sun and for screening from the next-door neighbours' yards. There is a narrow planting space between the pool and the brush fence on the northern side (facing south), a paved area abutting the house/garage wall on the southern side (facing north), with a number of planting holes left against the wall, while the rear western boundary incorporates a raised garden bed and dramatic water feature, backed by more brush fencing. Add to these physical constraints a tight budget (there is never much money left after you've put in a pool) and a brief for a tropical paradise, and you have a mini makeover that's quite a challenge.

TIMELINE Having brought in all the plants required, and vast quantities of potting mix (compost) and mulch (all bagged because of the difficult access), this makeover took three hours to complete, spending about an hour on each border. The first hour was spent on the north-facing wall, planting the bird of paradise (*Strelitzia reginae*). The second hour was taken up in planting the south-facing wall with the arum lilies, which needed dividing. The third hour was spent planting the western boundary with the variegated hibiscus and striking ruby-stemmed ginger, and potting up the frangipanis.

ONCE GROWN THESE HIBISCUS (HIBISCUS COOPERII) WILL FORM A STRIKING BACKDROP FOR THE SPLASHES OF RED-STEMMED GINGER, RED CENTRED BROMELIADS AND RED-FLOWERED HIBISCUS.

SUNNY WALL—STRELITZIA PLANTING

The north-facing southern side of the pool area, effectively a path from the house to the back of the garden, not only gets direct sun for the whole day (this is a southern hemisphere garden, and the reverse is true in the northern hemisphere), but also reflected sun and ambient heat from the light-coloured concrete-rendered wall behind it. Bird of paradise (*Strelitzia reginae*), so named because its magnificent flowerhead resembles a crested bird's head, is perfect for the small gaps left in the paving. Strelitzia cope extremely well with this sort of exposure, and flower throughout late summer, autumn and, most surprisingly, all winter. Their stylish grey-green leaves and fan-spray growth habit make them perfect for such a modern setting and narrow space; many other plants with similar architectural value have sharp points, which would be inappropriate next to a thoroughfare like this.

A larger species of strelitzia (*Strelitzia nicholai*), which has a similar leaf shape to the traveller's palm and striking ice-blue and white blooms, is transplanted into one corner to provide some screening from an encroaching building.

STEP 1

STEP 2

STEP 3

STEP 1   Divide potted strelitzias into smaller plants. You may have to exercise a bit of brute force here, with trowel and secateurs (garden shears), if the roots have curled around themselves.

STEP 2   Plant into holes and backfill with potting mix.

STEP 3   A selection of small succulents — chalksticks (*Senecio serpens*) and kalanchoe — underplanted in the pockets of soil will form a hardy groundcover. Mulch well and water in.

SHADY WALL—BRUSH FENCE

Finding plants to flower and look lush and tropical in a shady aspect is always tricky; add in the salt-water splash from this pool and you have an extra degree of difficulty in selecting the right plants.

The owners had some potted arum lilies they had brought with them from their previous house. These were divided up and planted along the northern fence line, and will provide stunning white blooms throughout winter (this being a southern hemisphere garden, a south-facing garden receives mostly shade). To add more height for screening, and for foliage contrast, we used a ginger with white-variegated leaves behind them. The front-row starring role is taken by the bright red New Guinea *Impatiens* 'Orange Neptis', which flowers virtually non-stop, is non-invasive and copes with a wider range of conditions than the regular types.

ARUM LILIES BEING REPLANTED   RED-FLOWERED NEW GUINEA IMPATIENS   WHITE VARIEGATED GINGER

NARROW WALL—RAISED BED

The raised bed against the rear boundary (facing east) needed an added 'wow' factor, as this is the main view seen from the house. A stepped pool wall (which houses the water feature) created an opportunity to feature some really special plants. Bright red-stemmed ginger (*Curcuma rubescens*) together with red-centred bromeliads (Neoregelia hybrid cultivars) make an eye-catching feature as the centrepiece, flanked by variegated hibiscus (*Hibiscus rosa-sinensis* var. *cooperii*), which copes with sun and shade, and has single bright red flowers, adding to the red theme threaded through the garden.

RED-CENTRED BROMELIADS HOLD POOLS OF WATER, WHICH CAN ENCOURAGE FROGS INTO THE GARDEN

WHILE EDIBLE GINGER IS GROWN IN MANY TROPICAL AREAS, THE BEAUTIFUL ORNAMENTAL FORMS ARE FINDING FAVOUR IN MANY GARDENS

A spare 5 minutes.

FINISHING TOUCHES

The other corner was planted with a small frangipani tree which, although deciduous, dropping both leaves and flowers, is considered well worth the maintenance for its superb fragrance and stunning orange-pink flowers. Matching frangipani plants were added in pots around the pool.

Frangipanis are perhaps the most evocative flowers around, reminiscent of lazy days beside a pool, perhaps on a tropical island. Although slow growing, they easily transplant and grow from cuttings, like the ones used here.

BEACH GARDEN

This backyard garden studio had everything it needed — running water, power, phone — everything except a garden. Transforming the narrow strip against the wall and the circular feature bed was an easy process, however, taking only half a day to complete once we had made the decision to keep with a beachside retro shack theme. This theme dictated the choice of plants, which had to be hardy and easy care, tolerant of heat and dryness, and happy to grow in sandy soil. A seaside-inspired colour scheme of aqua, white, yellow and brown was chosen, with ornaments and the details to complete the scene.

The plantings included a bougainvillea to grow against the back fence; a frangipani; glorious golden orange cannas and a cordyline underplanted with New Zealand flax (*Phormium* 'Surfer Boy') in the narrow bed against the wall (*Miscanthus* or *Pennisetum* would also work well), numerous succulents (echeverias, aloes and sedums, *Kalanchoe* 'Flap Jack' and *Graptonia* 'Debbie') to surround the water bowl taking pride of place in the round bed, and a selection of aquatics for the water bowl.

TIMELINE The first hour was spent clearing up and getting rid of fallen leaves, household junk and clutter. Painting the fence with whitewash and laying out the plants took up the second hour. It took another hour to plant out the potted plants and transplant others, while the fourth hour saw the water feature completed, the beds mulched and watered in, and lighting, deck chairs and other touches put in place.

CLEAN-UP, PAINTING AND POSITIONING

The first step here was to remove build-ups of old leaves, and the weeds poking up between the pavers, all of which were placed in the compost bin. Accumulated ancient and unwanted household junk and clutter stacked against walls and fences was given the heave-ho.

Next the walls were given a quick once-over with a soft broom to remove cobwebs, and leaves cleared from the roof, and walls and windows were hosed down and wiped over with a dry cloth. The paving was swept clean.

We decided to 'whitewash' the back fence, thus giving the timber a bleached look and adding to the seaside look. A white acrylic outdoor paint was watered down about half and half, and applied with a brush.

REMOVING COBWEBS, DIRT AND GRIME

SCRUBBING THE GRIME OFF PAVERS

WHITEWASHING THE BACK PAILING

PLANTING A SUCCULENT GARDEN

Succulents love to bask in the sun and will quite happily cope with a lack of water. What they don't like, however, is a rich organic soil mix or an overly shaded position. For this central feature bed it was important to make sure all organic debris was removed before planting (unusual in gardening, as you normally add organic matter) so that the succulents will not rot off.

STEP 1

STEP 2

STEP 3

HANDY HINT.

It any leaves break off, plant them, as they will quickly root and fill in the spaces with new plants.

STEP 4

STEP 5

STEP 1   Remove organic matter. Here, the top layer of rotting leaves is scraped off with a spade. It can be used elsewhere in the garden.

STEP 2   Dig the remaining soil over to check that it is friable and free draining.

STEP 3   Starting with the largest plants, in this case Aloe, begin planting. Care must be taken with any top-heavy plants to support their upper parts while planting — they can easily break off.

STEP 4   Plant the smaller, groundcovering types of succulent, like these echeverias and sedums.

STEP 5   To add to the beachside feel, sand is used to top-dress the garden bed.

PLANTING A WATER FEATURE

Just like a garden in the ground, plant choice for a water feature will vary depending on the position. Iris, water lilies and water poppies need plenty of sun (at least 5 or 6 hours a day) in order to flower. Other flowering aquatics, such as arum lilies, will cope easily in the shade. For a more textural garden use grasses instead: dwarf papyrus, striped sedges and colourful carex all grow well in both sunshine and shade. Floating aquatics, like duckweed and fairy moss (*Azolla caroliniana*), can also be used, but as these grow very quickly, only include them if you intend to regularly remove (and destroy thoughtfully) the excess plants. Keeping goldfish in the pond will control mosquito larvae.

You can choose to plant the aquatics directly into the water bowl or simply arrange them, still potted. Each method has its advantages. Potted plants are easily removed and replaced as the need arises, but have less available root-zone and will need more frequent repotting.

STEP 1

STEP 2

STEP 3

S T E P 1   Make sure the water bowl is level. Use sand to create a level base if the bowl is placed in a garden. If you are planting directly into the bowl, add a 20 cm (8 in) layer of potting mix, plant, and cover the soil with a layer of heavy pebbles. Half-fill the bowl with water, VERY slowly if you have put soil in.

S T E P 2   Some sedge that was growing in another part of the garden was potted up in three plastic pots, and some tall reeds were planted directly into the bowl. Placing pebbles around potted aquatics helps stop soil from floating up to the surface of the water, and weighs the pots down, helping to anchor them in place.

S T E P 3   Slowly add water until the pond is nearly full.

GARDENER'S TIP. A green algae sometimes occurs in pond water, but it is only a problem if it causes excess greening of the water. Causes include excessively alkaline water or lack of oxygenating plants. Condy's crystals (¼ teaspoon per bucket), dissolved, then added to pond water can be used to treat infestations. Or simply use a stick and pull out excess strands.

A few goldfish will quickly keep mosquito larvae under control. Add some water-purifying agent if you are going to have goldfish, as per directions on the bottle, then add the fish.

FENCED IN

Having whitewashed the back fence with a white wash, the time to dress it up has arrived. Pale aqua-blue paint was added to diagonal lattice, then hung simply like a picture onto a few nails. This forms the support for a transplanted lilac-coloured bougainvillea, which will enjoy the reflected light. Gazanias and agapanthus carpet the ground level.

STEP 1

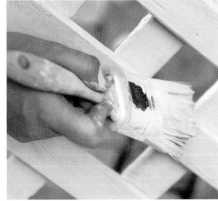

STEP 2

STEP 3

STEP 4

STEP 5

STEP 1   This bougainvillea was carefully dug up from another part of the garden. Thorough watering immediately will ensure its survival.

STEP 2   An acrylic aqua-toned paint adds to the seaside theme and is simple to apply with a brush.

STEP 3   By hammering in a few nails, you can easily hang (and remove) your lattice panel.

STEP 4   Fitting the panel.

STEP 5   Twisties (plastic-coated wire) hold the bougainvillea tendrils in place while it establishes itself.

BEACH BOYS

This garden is home to two teenage boys who love the surf — and so to accomodate their hobby into the scene, the trick was to add to the boards with other things reminiscent of the 'beach boys' era. Popular plants of the day, like 'Bobby Dazzler' petunias, New Zealand cabbage trees (*Cordyline*) and canna lilies with their wild variegated leaves just seem to 'fit' the right image. Add to this their adaptability to sandy soils and you have a themed garden that fits the scene perfectly.

TRANSPLANTING A CORDYLINE

PETUNIA 'BOBBY DAZZLER'

BROMELIADS ADD COLOUR AND DRAMA

A *spare* 5 *minutes*.

FINISHING TOUCHES

Colourful lanterns completed the look in this retro garden. Simple self-adhesive hooks take less than one minute to attach under the eaves, and the lanterns are just as simple to assemble.

SANCTUARY

A few boulders in the backyard might not be everyone's idea of the perfect garden, but treated the right way even the most difficult space can be transformed into a delightful garden sanctuary. Everyone wishes for a little peace and tranquillity at times, but finding space for contemplation is often difficult. Carving a niche in the garden is easier than finding a private space in the house, however, so try creating a sanctuary out of doors.

The rocks in this lightly-shaded nook are softened with age and moss, and combine well with the sea of maidenhair fern, cool, serene and green, frothing around their bases. A potted mini-garden of golden sedge grass and moss-like mounds of saxifrage (*Saxifraga maderiensis*) and two white-glazed feature planters with rippled sides, holding stunning cycads, enhance the effect. A float bowl filled with pebbles, flowers or candles would be a lovely extra touch. A comfortable folding chair and, if necessary, a free-standing bamboo screen for privacy, complete an intimate space for one. The key is simplicity and easy care — you don't want to be a slave to the garden space that is your sanctuary.

A VERY ZEN COMPOSITION WHERE THE SIMPLICITY OF SEDGE GRASS AND SAXIFRAGE SPEAKS FOR ITSELF

CYCADS WERE AROUND WITH THE DINOSAURS, BUT LOOK JUST AS COMFORTABLE TODAY

ENCHANTED

Purple works particularly well at dusk taking on an enchanted feel as the sun sets. You can easily capitalize on this with the addition of some simple candles and a throw, all in soft lavender and lilac tones. Add some sparkle with sequins or beads, or even pots with opalescent glazes, and you have a magical scene conjured up in minutes.

JUST FOR FUN

Sometimes it's nice just to have some fun in the garden, and not take yourself too seriously. In days gone by, follies were sometimes incorporated into large country estates for much the same reason. Today, your garden folly might be a garden gnome or a pink flamingo, but more stylish and functional options, such as an outdoor shower or even bath, a hammock, a few candles or a bamboo screen or flower float bowl may be just the props needed to encourage you to sit back and relax, or have a little giggle!

HANGING A HAMMOCK

YOU will Need.

Hammock

2 pigtail bolts with washer plates and nuts

Drill

Ring spanner or small shifter

Lying around in a hammock is a wonderful way to enjoy the garden! But the first thing you need for hanging a hammock is a suitable host. A tree with a low-lying horizontal branch would be most people's ideal site, but you can't always find a truly horizontal branch. Don't despair — you can add hammock springs between the attachment points of tree and hammock to even out the inequality, as long as the difference in height is not too great. But a word of caution here — not all trees are suitable candidates for hanging hammocks. Avoid brittle-timbered trees such as robinias and coral trees — you don't want to find yourself (or your child or your guest) pinned to the ground by a large branch. Mature specimens of trees such as willows, elms, Moreton Bay figs and Hills figs are usually the best choice. Your other options in the event of not having a suitable tree are to hang the hammock from a pergola or between two posts, or to use a self-supporting hammock stand.

STEP 1

STEP 2

STEP 3

STEP 4

STEP 5

STEP 1   When you've found the right tree and the right branch, work out where you want to sling the hammock and drill a hole for the first pigtail bolt using the appropriate-sized bit.

STEP 2   Work a pigtail bolt (these bolts are the sort you use for hanging swings in trees) through the hole.

STEP 3   Add the washer plate and screw the nut on firmly.

STEP 4   Measure out the required distance to the second hole by attaching one end of the hammock to the fixed pigtail, and stretching it out until it is far enough off the ground. Mark the point for the second pigtail and drill the hole.

STEP 5   Repeat steps 2 and 3, then hang the other end of the hammock. Lie back and enjoy — that is, if you can beat the kids in the rush.

FLAT-PACK FURNITURE

Creating a place to eat outdoors has now become almost more important than the garden itself, which is no surprise given the relaxing atmosphere alfresco dining creates and the ease with which one can extend the house and create an outdoor dining room. This courtyard space, situated under a pergola, was certainly a lot easier to make into a dining room than extending the house, with the only construction work involved being an easy-to-assemble flat pack of outdoor timber furniture. A few pots filled with maples, a surrounding box hedge contained in a raised planter box and a table dressed with mondo grass complete the setting.

GAR*den*er's *tip.* Always make sure that wooden furniture is placed on a hard surface, like brickwork. Earthern or grass floors may look nice, but moisture soon finds its way up through the cut grain ends of the legs and will cause rot.

FURNITURE

This hardwood furniture is bought in a flat pack and comes together simply. The holes are pre-drilled, and the screws fastened with an allen key.

Outdoor timber furniture is a unique product, creating a wonderful natural look that can be both contemporary and rustic. It comes with various ratings for durability, with 1 being the highest score (for hardwoods like spotted gum) for its strength and wear, meaning that it is suitable for a variety of outdoor uses, from verandah posts to rails, decking and bridges.

To keep hardwood furniture in good shape, you are best treating it with oil on a regular basis, say every winter. Furniture that has gone too long between 'drinks' might need to be sanded back lightly first.

STEP 1

STEP 2

STEP 3

STEP 1   Wash timber with water and a light bristle brush.

STEP 2   When dry, apply the appropriate oil with a brush. The grade of oil you use will depend on whether the furniture sits out in the garden or receives some protection on a verandah or patio.

STEP 3   Allow the oil to soak in for 10 minutes, then wipe off the excess with a clean, dry rag. Dry overnight. The next day, apply another coat and again wipe off the excess after 10 minutes and allow to dry overnight.

OUTDOOR SHOWER

Embracing the great outdoors (at least, for those of us blessed with a mild climate) can have its drawbacks, among which are the dirt and grime that nature is full of. Whether it be sand from the beach, dirt from the garden or just the accumulated sweat from a hard day's work, walking it into the house has its problems – especially for the person who has to clean the bathroom! Installing an outdoor shower is a simple solution, and easy to do in less than an hour. Kit showers are available from some hardware shops and homemaker centres. They connect up to the garden tap for an invigorating wash after work or a quick rinse-off after a dip in the pool.

Choose your location carefully. Make sure you can easily get to a tap, or purchase a hose long enough to reach your intended spot. So that water doesn't pool around the shower, choose a position that is sufficiently elevated to allow run-off to get away, otherwise you'll have to install drainage. Gravel is a great surround material for an outdoor shower, because it is so porous and stays clean. It can be a bit hard on bare feet, though, so a few timber decking squares laid over the gravel make a good compromize.

YOU WiLL NeeD.

Outdoor shower kit

Screwdriver

Plumber's tape

STEP 1

STEP 2

STEP 3

STEP 4

STEP 5

STEP 6

S T E P   1   Read the instructions that come with the kit carefully, and check you have all the pieces that are supposed to be included. The kit I used comes with a ready-assembled base plate of timber decking, but everything else I had to put together myself, including the plumbing components. Lay the base plate on the most suitable spot.

S T E P   2   Insert the dowel into the uprights which form the bottom part of the stand for the shower pipe. Firmly tap the pieces together with your palms until they are locked into position.

S T E P   3   Screw the stand to the underside of the base plate using the pre-drilled holes and support pieces.

S T E P   4   Fit the top part of the shower stand by matching the pre-drilled holes together and screwing in the screws supplied. This completes the wooden frame.

S T E P   5   Assembling the plumbing is simple, as there are only a few components to be connected. The important points here are to make sure that the washers are in place, and that you use plenty of plumber's tape around each connection so that there are no leaks.

S T E P   6   Screw the soap holder in position. Now you can connect a garden hose and enjoy the prospect of less dirt coming into the house.

INDEX

Published in 2006 by Murdoch Books Pty Limited
www.murdochbooks.com.au

Murdoch Books Australia
Pier 8/9, 23 Hickson Road
Millers Point NSW 2000
Phone: +61 (0) 2 8220 2000
Fax: +61 (0) 2 8220 2558

Murdoch Books UK Limited
Erico House, 6th Floor North
93–99 Upper Richmond Road
Putney, London SW15 2TG
Phone: +44 (0) 20 8785 5995
Fax: +44 (0) 20 8785 5985

National Library of Australia Cataloguing-in-Publication Data

Kirton, Meredith, 1969- .
An hour in the garden.

Includes index.
ISBN 978 1 74045 822 1.

ISBN 1 74045 822 2.

1. Gardening - Australia - Handbooks, manuals, etc. 2.
Gardens - Australia. I. Title.

635.0994

Chief Executive: Juliet Rogers
Publishing Director: Kay Scarlett

Design manager: Vivien Valk
Design concept: Sarah Odgers
Designers: Susanne Geppert, Sarah Odgers
Project manager: Emma Hutchinson
Editor: Anne Savage
Photographer: Sue Stubbs
Production: Maiya Levitch

Printed by 1010 Printing International Limited in 2006.
PRINTED IN CHINA.

Text © Meredith Kirton 2006
Design © Murdoch Books Pty Limited 2006
Photography © Sue Stubbs 2006

Readers of this book must ensure that any work or
project undertaken complies with local legislative and approval
requirements relevant to their particular circumstances.
Furthermore, this work is necessarily of a general nature
and cannot be a substitute for appropriate professional advice.